3/97

UNIVERSITY OF
WOLVERHAMPTON

LR/LEND/002

ONE WEEK LOAN

1 0 NOV 1999   1 1 DEC 2000

2 1 FEB 2000   1 8 APR 2002

2 9 FEB 2000   1 1 MAR 2003

- 9 MAR 2000   - 2 DEC 2003

1 6 MAR 2000   - 5 FEB 2008

2 2 MAR 2000   9 NOV 2010

Telephone Renewals: 01902 321333
Please RETURN this item on or before the last date shown above.
Fines will be charged if items are returned late.
See tariff of fines displayed at the Counter.   (L2)

CHILDREN OF SILENCE

CHILDREN OF SILENCE

The story of Sarah and Joanne's triumph
over deafness

KATHY ROBINSON

LONDON
VICTOR GOLLANCZ LTD
1987

First published in Great Britain
by Victor Gollancz Ltd
14 Henrietta St London WC2E 8QJ

British Library Cataloguing in Publication Data
Robinson, Kathy
  Children of silence.
  1. Children, Deaf – Language 2. Children,
  Deaf – Family relationships 3. Parent
  and child
  I. Title
  401'.9   HV2483
  ISBN 0-575-03908-6

Note

Certain names in this book have been changed, and conversations,
while as accurate as they possibly can be, are still from memory.

Photoset in Great Britain by
Rowland Phototypesetting Ltd, Bury St Edmunds, Suffolk
and printed by St Edmundsbury Press Ltd
Bury St Edmunds, Suffolk

*I dedicate this book
to all parents everywhere*

Acknowledgements

I would like to thank, in particular, my friend Kath Moodie for her much needed support and encouragement throughout the writing of this book; Carmel Hayward for our stimulating conversations and her reading and approval of the script; my aunt Joan – also for reading and approving the script – my gratitude always; my sister Julie for her fingers (until I learnt to type); my mother and father for their belief in me; Mona Mitchell for being there; Elfreda Powell, editor at Gollancz, whose guidance made the cutting of 40,000 words less harrowing than it might otherwise have been; Joan Ayling for quite simply everything; Pauline, a very special person; certain professionals who gave me much of their valuable time; our relations for providing the loving family unit in which Sarah and Joanne have grown, but especially Mick's sister, Margaret, and Grandma to whom we owe so much; Jimmy and Barbara for their friendship and hospitality; the many teachers who have cared, and still continue to care, for the welfare of Sarah and Joanne; Sarah and Joanne's friends who are truly marvellous; and finally Mick whose forbearance in the writing (and rewriting and rewriting . . .) of this book was quite exceptional.

To you all, and the many others I have been unable to mention, I say a heartfelt 'Thank you'.

K.R.

Contents

1.   *The appointment*

AN APPOINTMENT HAS BEEN MADE FOR SARAH
ROBINSON AT ... HOSPITAL ON 23RD
SEPTEMBER AT 2 00 P.M. PLEASE CONFIRM.

'Sarah.'

I spoke my two-and-a-half-year-old daughter's name quietly in the waiting room. I called her name again, louder this time, and when she did not turn towards me, fear clutched at my heart.

Conscious that all eyes were upon me, I said 'Sarah' once more and raised my hand to touch her shoulder, but she turned round with a quizzical smile on her face as if to say she knew I had been calling her all the time. The summer sun had lightened her hair and wispy curls were beginning to form. Her skin had a translucent sheen, one or two freckles dotted her nose, and there was an intent look in her luminous blue eyes as though she knew that today was especially important.

Before long two small children began to run round the room and Sarah waited for them to indicate that she could join in. After a while her laughter, higher in pitch than the children's, began to resound disturbingly in my head.

Outwardly I appeared calm. If the months of waiting for this appointment had taught me anything, it was control. Unable to translate my anxiety into words, I suppressed my fear. But something bad was going to happen soon. I knew it. Something really bad.

Sarah's white lacy tights were wrinkled at the knee and I smoothed them out with my hand. She was wearing a new red dress with a navy collar to match the navy band down the front. Sometimes I wondered if it was wrong to love someone as much as I loved her. She touched something deep within me yet I didn't seem able to reach her in the same way. There was an elusive quality about her.

An hour passed and the numbers in the waiting-room dwindled until only a man and his young son remained in the row in front of us. The man turned around and smiled and I said, 'Why are you here?'

'My son's having his six-monthly check-up,' he replied. 'My wife's in there with him now.' Then he added by way of explanation: 'My other son is deaf.'

His words were unexpected. I wanted to say I was sorry but didn't know if that was the right thing to do. He was about thirty and everything about him suggested he was a professional man. I couldn't believe he could have a deaf son.

'I hope you've had help with him,' I said, unable to envisage the kind of help a deaf child might need.

The man turned in his chair to face me more fully, and I sensed he was pleased by my interest. 'Well, until recently we lived in America but we came home to have my son educated in England. We didn't want him to use sign language as they do in the schools over there. We wanted him to learn to speak.'

I nodded, encouraging him to continue.

'The school's been very good,' he went on, 'and we're pleased with his progress. We used to work with him at home but now we do less than we ever did.' He looked towards Sarah. 'Why are you here?'

For a moment we sat and watched Sarah engrossed in the task of interlocking some plastic shapes together. The effort had caused a pink flush to come to her cheeks.

The man waited for my answer unaware of the panic ballooning inside me. 'Sarah's not talking yet and we think she has fluid in her ears which is blocking the sound,' I said. 'A friend of mine had the same problem with her daughter.'

At first I had thought Sarah wasn't talking because I was anticipating her every need, but, when I tried pretending I didn't understand what she wanted, she had screamed and banged her head on the floor with frustration. Then I thought perhaps it was because *I* had been a late talker. And my neighbour told me her little boy was three before he said a word.

Finally I took her to the doctor at the baby clinic who said he would refer her to an Ear, Nose and Throat specialist. Day after day I had tested Sarah's hearing myself. I dropped keys behind her back and she didn't turn. I dropped keys behind her back and she *did* turn. I was sick with worry and the waiting was dreadful because Sarah was so unhappy.

I looked at the man again. 'She's so quick and she understands everything I say.'

Almost immediately I regretted my insensitivity. I might just as well have said that I didn't think Sarah was like his son.

'She certainly seems aware,' the man smiled at Sarah.

Before he could say more, an attractive auburn-haired woman came into the room closely followed by a boy of about seven. He had dark hair like his father and small delicate features. I couldn't equate deafness with him – not until his mother bent to straighten his tie and I caught a glimpse of an ugly black hearing-aid beneath his school blazer.

'YOU WERE A VERY GOOD BOY. MUMMY'S VERY PLEASED WITH YOU,' the woman said loudly, stressing every syllable. She opened her handbag and gave the boy a packet of sweets without so much as a glance in the direction of her husband and other son.

The boy began to speak. His voice was flat and gutteral, his words unintelligible.

As the family were leaving I heard a voice behind me say, 'Mrs Robinson?' Sarah swung round to look at the nurse and without a moment's hesitation climbed down from my knee and took the hand that was outstretched to her. I was aware of the tapping of Sarah's red shoes as we went down the corridor, and the click of my high heels: ordinary comforting sounds.

We came to a room where several people were standing beneath a bright fluorescent light. They were talking to each other, oblivious of our presence. I reached for Sarah's hand and held it tightly. Why were all these people here? I had expected a specialist and a nurse perhaps. Suddenly I was out of my depth. There were no signposts now.

The group divided and a man moved forward to welcome us. 'Hello Mrs Robinson. Hello Sarah.' I smiled and shook his hand wondering why he was dressed in a suit instead of a white coat.

'Is your husband with you? He's welcome to come in as well.'

'No, he's looking after our other daughter. Joanne's only a baby,' I explained.

'I'm Mr Chapman and this is . . .' He introduced me to the occupants of the room, a courtesy unknown in my experience of hospitals.

'If you would sit here Mrs Robinson.' Mr Chapman indicated a chair in the centre of the room. 'Will you put Sarah on your knee and try not to move or touch her. If you would put your arms down by your side,' he suggested.

Sarah sat stiffly on my knee, every sense alert. She had the same serious look she always had in new situations. It was almost as though she must absorb every single detail to store in her memory, and sometimes when I looked at her, I imagined a secret life sheltering behind her eyes, a life which I could never penetrate.

'We're going to test Sarah's hearing,' Mr Chapman informed me. 'The test material will contain a range of high and low sounds found in speech.'

I resisted the impulse to tell him Sarah had already had her hearing tested when she was a baby, since he had her medical records.

A smartly dressed woman came to sit on the floor in front of our chair. She waved a toy and when Sarah looked towards her, she hid the toy with her hand. Just then Mr Chapman rustled some paper behind us very quietly.

I waited for Sarah to react but she made no attempt to turn. I longed to move my leg to tell her what she was supposed to do.

'That was the low frequency sound. Now we'll try the high frequency one.'

The testing continued. Each time Sarah turned to a sound Mr Chapman patted her on the shoulder. He even patted her when she turned at a different time to the sound. When he began stroking the inside of a cup with a spoon, Sarah must have felt me willing her to turn because she spun round immediately. I breathed a sigh of relief.

But Mr Chapman laughed. 'We've a bright one here,' he said. 'Sarah saw my assistant look at me when I scraped the spoon against the cup and she followed the look to me.'

The significance of his remark escaped me.

Twenty minutes passed and still we had not finished. Sarah was led to a small desk and chair. On the desk was a wooden boat with eight little men standing beside it.

'This will determine the level at which Sarah hears low frequency sound.' Mr Chapman crouched before her and smiled. To show her what he wanted her to do he put one of the men in her hand, said 'Go,' then guided it towards the boat.

Sarah placed the man inside it.

'Very-good-girl,' Mr Chapman spoke slowly and clearly. Sarah wriggled in her seat at his praise.

Why didn't he let her play with the toys now? She had done so well. The atmosphere was beginning to frighten me.

Mr Chapman went behind Sarah and said 'Go' near her right ear.

Sarah waited, her body still poised for the signal.

Mr Chapman tried again. He shouted 'Go!' at the top of his voice and the word reverberated around the room.

Sarah leaned forward and put the man in the boat.

I wanted to hug her. She had done what he wanted her to do.

'Go.' Mr Chapman lowered his voice to a more normal level.

Sarah waited.

'Go!' Mr Chapman shouted as loudly as he had done before.

I caught the flicker of a smile as Sarah placed the man firmly in the boat. Then she sat back pleased with herself.

'That's the threshold of her hearing,' Mr Chapman said to a woman in a white coat. He crossed the room and shouted the same loud 'Go!' into a sound-level meter standing on a table. Turning to me he explained, 'That's where Sarah begins to hear low-frequency sound.'

We had been here for three-quarters of an hour now and Sarah was still co-operating. Mr Chapman had a way with children and he injected enthusiasm into every move he made.

The assistant took over the testing for Sarah's left ear. She shouted 'Go!' but no matter how hard she tried she couldn't shout the word loudly enough. 'I can't get any louder,' she said to Mr Chapman with a note of disappointment. I wondered if Sarah was being purposely contrary.

Mr Chapman began again. He shouted 'Go!' repeatedly until he was exhausted. Eventually he crossed the room to the sound-level meter saying: 'That's her threshold.'

The tension in Sarah was transmitting itself to me. She didn't have to tell me she was losing patience, I could sense every change of mood in her. Her feelings were my feelings. It had always been like that.

Mr Chapman started to test Sarah with something he called a pure tone audiometer. I could see what he was doing without it registering in my mind. I felt very alone. Insignificant almost. Despite every attempt Mr Chapman had made to include me, I felt excluded. Sarah had started fidgeting and glancing in my direction. It was too much to expect her to sit here any longer.

The testing came to a halt and the equipment was put away. Then Mr Chapman came to sit beside me. A hush descended upon the room and I had a sudden desire to put my hands over my ears before he could say anything. I found it disconcerting to have him sitting so close, and his eyes seemed able to penetrate the fear in my mind. The room was heavy with apprehension. I heard Sarah playing with the toy boat. Wood knocked on wood. A handbag clicked. Someone blew their nose. A throat cleared.

'Mrs Robinson.'

. . .

'Mrs Robinson, Sarah's hearing is seriously impaired.'

Mr Chapman's expression was one of deep concern. He continued speaking, but I didn't hear him. What was he saying? Too soon his words slotted into place. He was saying Sarah wasn't like I thought she was – a hearing child.

He was saying she was *deaf*.

But what was deafness? What did it look like? How did it feel? Frantically I searched for some image, a picture of deafness – then I thought of the boy in the waiting-room.

The picture changed to a warm sunny afternoon in May when Mick and I brought Sarah out of the nursing home where she was born. So many new emotions had merged with the excitement that day. Sarah was strong and healthy and she had the biggest bluest eyes I had ever seen.

The weeks had flown by. Sarah struggled first to raise her head, to sit, to grasp with both hands, and then to crawl. She drank from a cup, built bricks, and learned to stand, all much sooner than most other babies.

Once, when she was five months old, I took her on a train journey and to keep her occupied I showed her how to sort buttons into sizes, play finger rhymes, and thread beads on to a string. At the end of the trip a lady came up to me and said, 'You have a very bright little baby there.'

I thought of Sarah at eleven months taking her first faltering steps into Mick's arms in the garden of my parents' bungalow.

Then Sarah at fourteen months in a white dress running towards me down the hall of our house as I carried Joanne, a tiny bundle, home for the first time.

And Sarah at two with her friends on the beach: playful, mischievous and full of fun.

From deep down inside I felt the tears welling. I had lost Sarah. Lost the Sarah I knew.

Sarah was *deaf*!

Everything added up now: Sarah's crying when she was a baby because she didn't want to be left alone; afterwards, her frustration and tantrums. She was telling me something was wrong but the invisibility of her deafness had meant I failed to recognize what that 'something' was. Now I knew why she seemed so unfeeling. Deafness had been an ever-present barrier between us.

I had thought that Sarah was being disobedient when she wouldn't do as she was told. Once I called her name as she ran down the road and when she 'refused' to stop, I smacked her leg. I hadn't understood it when she turned towards me with a surprised and hurt expression.

Deafness had been the reason for her independence. She'd had to rely on herself because she couldn't rely on other people. She had become a fighter because she'd had to fight to survive.

Could I ever make up for what I had done to her?

'Why did it happen?' I held back my tears afraid that Mr Chapman would become impatient with me.

'Did you have any problems with pregnancy?'

It all came flooding back to me. 'I had a threatened miscarriage, and I was in contact with German measles before I knew I was pregnant.'

'Rubella.' Mr Chapman nodded at the woman in the white coat as if he found this significant.

'I had a blood test though. My doctor said anti-bodies were present and I had no need to worry.'

Mr Chapman had moved from my side and I felt abandoned. Everyone was getting ready to go home.

'Sarah passed her hearing test,' I said. As far as I was concerned the test stated that Sarah's hearing was normal. I had thought it was infallible.

Mr Chapman frowned. 'I'm afraid we have a long way to go in perfecting our methods of screening for hearing.'

'Why didn't I know?'

'Well, for a start, you wouldn't have been expecting Sarah to have a hearing loss and she is a first child. Besides she would have responded to stimuli other than sound: a vibration, a reflection in a mirror, a draught as a door opens. . . .' He hesitated. 'I don't know whether you are aware of it but you sign to Sarah.'

Yesterday I had asked Sarah to fetch a cloth from the kitchen and she had run to get it for me. I thought she had heard me but she must have seen the milk spilt, my 'rubbing' gesture and pointed finger.

'I thought the tonsillitis Sarah gets had caused a temporary loss of hearing,' I said. 'My doctor told me she would grow out of it.'

'Sarah has a sensori-neural loss of hearing or nerve deafness,' Mr Chapman explained.

'Is there anything that can be done? An operation?'

'There isn't a cure for nerve deafness.'

Somehow I knew the answer before I had asked the question.

'What can I do? How can I help her?' I needed to think I could do something. An idea came to me. 'Could I train to be a teacher of the deaf?'

'Don't worry about that for now,' Mr Chapman replied. 'What we're going to do Mrs Robinson is to give Sarah a hearing-aid. That's the first thing. Then you will begin seeing a teacher of the deaf who will help you. You're lucky. We're starting a clinic in your area next month.'

Next month! What would I do for a whole month?

There was one more question I had to ask and it couldn't be withheld any longer.

'Will Sarah learn to talk?'

There was no reply.

The assistant had been waiting for me by the door and, taking Sarah's hand, I followed her into the corridor and on to the next stage. Sarah's shoes tapped lightly on the tiled floor again as she skipped by my side. She couldn't hear the sound they made. I ached all over. One long ache of despair.

We were led into a room where a young girl in a white coat said, 'We'll take an impression of Sarah's ear so that we can make her an ear mould.' I held Sarah's hand to reassure her as a soft pink substance was pressed into her ear.

'It's better if you can cry,' the assistant said. 'Would you like me to ring your husband?'

'No, I'll be all right. Thank you though.'

'Here's Sarah's hearing-aid,' she said, placing it in my hand. I looked down at the black box. *It was identical to the one the boy in the waiting-room had worn.*

At last we were free to go, and Sarah and I walked to the car park. The sun was shining and the sky an unending blue. Once upon a time I had thought nothing bad could happen on a sunny day.

Sarah ran ahead of me to the car, a trim little figure without a care in the world. I expected her to have changed somehow, but she looked the same. She didn't seem to be deaf in the way the boy in the waiting-room had been.

As I unlocked the door of the car to let her in, a bird sang in the tree above me. Lorries rumbled past the exit of the hospital. All around me were sounds I had paid scant attention to before; now they had the power to overwhelm me with sadness. I thought of everything Sarah would miss as if she had become deaf today and not before she was born: the sound of running water, singing, the lap of waves on the shore, a clock ticking. . . . What about the television and the radio?

And oh – she would never hear my voice.

There were only two stages in my life now: before knowing about Sarah's deafness and after. Did Mr Chapman realize what his words had done? They had changed our lives for ever.

Before, we were an ordinary family. Now, deafness had come to set us apart and make us different. We were on our own. Alone.

But the effects deafness would have on Mick and myself were minor considerations when compared to the consequences for Sarah. Would it mean a life of deprivation, not only of sound but everything else as well? Would it mean she would never play tennis, go to a dance, attend university? What about having a boyfriend, getting married, and rearing children?

Had Sarah been robbed of her life, the life she would have had had she not been deaf? And had we been robbed of it too?

I had arranged to meet Mick at his sister's house but, as I turned the corner near where she lived, he was walking towards us. I stopped the car and he opened the door.

'I was just going to the shop,' he said as he sat down. '. . . What is it? What's wrong?' His calm and gentle expression changed and his eyes moved quickly to Sarah to check she was all right, then they returned to me.

I was in control by now yet detached from everything that was going on. I didn't feel compassion towards Mick as I should have done, I just felt numb.

I tried to soften my words, then watched as if from a distance as he put his head in his hands and said, 'Oh no,' over and over again before turning in his seat to touch Sarah and say her name.

At Mick's sister's house I went into the lounge to look for Joanne: even though she was only fourteen months old, she was the only one who could bring me comfort. When she saw me walk into the room her face broke into a huge smile and she lifted up her arms wanting me to hold her. I buried my head in the sweet-smelling folds of her cardigan and she put her arms round my neck making funny gurgling noises. No child could ever have been as loving as she. Her soft cheek pressed against mine and she patted my head, a wicked look in her eye. She looked so pretty that somehow my sense of despair was heightened.

'Is there an operation?'

'No.'

'There must be.'

'There isn't. There's nothing they can do medically.'

'What caused it?'

'They can't be certain.'

One at a time Mick's mother and sister came into the lounge to look at Sarah and ask questions. They kept saying it wasn't possible, and not to worry, as if someone had made a big mistake. I didn't want to be here answering their questions, I wanted to be miles and miles from anywhere. Not for one moment did I take their feelings into account, for they loved Sarah too. They were the best kind of family to have, but I couldn't share this with them. This terrible thing had happened to *me*. Sarah was sitting on the floor smothered in chocolate. It hadn't taken her long to realize the atmosphere was in her favour – and to take advantage of it.

'It'll get better,' Grandma said. 'You'll see. She'll grow out of it.'

2.   A *toy merry-go-round*

The month in which we waited for the appointment with the teacher of the deaf passed slowly. When the day finally arrived Sarah and I made our way to the clinic three miles from where we lived.

We entered a square hallway and through one of the doors leading off it, I saw a lady sitting opposite a small boy who was holding a feather between his teeth. Sarah would soon be doing that, I thought. Learning how to pronounce words properly.

Another door opened and as the teacher ushered a small girl from her room, my heart jumped when I saw her black hearing-aid. It was strapped to her chest, blatantly ruining the front of her dress.

The teacher greeted me and said 'Hello' to Sarah. She was well-groomed and self-assured, and this made me feel even worse than I had before. If Sarah needed a professional like this to help her, what could I possibly have to offer? She had a specialist knowledge of deaf children and I had none.

Sarah was asked to sit at a small table upon which stood a machine and a pair of earphones. The teacher placed the earphones over Sarah's head and adjusted them to fit her ears tightly. She switched the machine on and spoke into a microphone which hung from a cord around her neck. 'One, two, three. Hello, hello. Testing. Testing.' When she was satisfied it was working she looked up at me. 'This is an auditory training unit,' she explained. 'It amplifies sound. I can adjust it to suit Sarah's hearing loss. This knob here boosts the high tones, and this the low tones. That dial there tells me how loud my voice is. I have to keep it on a level which makes the needle stay on the red line.'

I watched the needle as it wavered near the red line, and saw it fall when the teacher stopped speaking. Sarah was fascinated too. It surprised me she hadn't made a fuss about wearing the earphones. They were far too large and cumbersome for a child.

'If you watch everything I do,' the teacher went on, 'then you'll be able to copy the session at home with Sarah.' She held the microphone near her mouth. 'Hello *Sarah.*'

. . . I moved forward in my chair to interrupt. I would have to explain that Sarah didn't know her name. I had been saying 'Sarah' for years. Surely she realized that Sarah couldn't hear.

On the floor by the teacher's side was a large cardboard box, and, as the lesson progressed, she pulled pieces of a toy merry-go-round from it and joined them together with gaily painted nuts and bolts. I concentrated on every move she made. I noticed she spoke clearly and that she held the pieces of the merry-go-round up near her mouth.

'Here's a stick,' she said. 'A long stick.' She traced her finger slowly across it, then added, 'I'll *push* the stick through the hole.' She pretended to find this difficult to do but as Sarah reached out to help her, she drew the stick back up to her mouth. 'You *push* it through the hole,' she said.

She passed the stick to Sarah and when Sarah had pushed it through the hole, she took it away from her again.

Sarah looked deflated.

'You don't have to exaggerate your words though it will be a temptation to do so,' the teacher said. 'But you must speak clearly and in short sentences. When you get home try practising in the mirror. If you put a slight emphasis on the key words it will help Sarah, but you must keep them in the context of a sentence, otherwise Sarah won't learn words like "the, through, and, round, in," and these are important for the sense of the sentence. At the beginning you'll find "action" words will be easier for Sarah to understand because she will see their movements. So try using words like "pushing, pulling, running," and "jumping".'

I stared at her, mesmerized by her glossy pink lips, and tried to make sense of it all. As far as I could tell Sarah wasn't understanding anything that was being said to her. As for me, it was like trying to learn a foreign language. Why wasn't Sarah being taught to say words? Why did the teacher put earphones on her? Why couldn't Sarah play with the toys?

'If you bring the toys up to your mouth it will encourage Sarah to watch your lips for information,' the teacher's voice interrupted my thoughts. 'Some people call it face-reading because information is gained from the whole face and not just the lips.'

Information. What information? I tried to look as if I understood the whole magical process, a process which was so far removed from my experience that it was impossible for me to understand.

'Why can't Sarah play with the toys?' I asked.

'Because she would be looking at them and not at your face.'

I was pleased with Sarah. She looked calm but I knew that, inside, she was like a taut ball of wire, waiting to spring. It would happen. After we had left the teacher's presence Sarah's frustration would find release.

'Here's a horse. It's got some *eyes*.' The teacher pointed to the horse's eyes and then her own. 'The horse has a *nose*. You have a *nose*.' She touched Sarah on the tip of her nose. Sarah stiffened.

The lesson dragged on interminably until the merry-go-round was complete. At last Sarah could play and I could ask the questions I had stored for over a month.

'Will Sarah have to go to boarding school?' This had worried me so much I hadn't been able to sleep.

The teacher helped Sarah to undo the screw on the merry-go-round before she answered me. 'Some Authorities do make boarding school placements but we think a child should be helped by the mother in the home. You see, if parents learn to help their children from the beginning, their support usually continues right through the child's education. When Sarah starts school she will go to the School for the Deaf.'

Then I asked the question which had tormented me even more. 'Will Sarah learn to talk?' That was all I wanted to know. In the last month I had alternated between thinking deafness was a handicap of immense proportion, or a sad, but nevertheless minor, inconvenience.

The teacher drew in her breath as if she was preparing herself for something unpleasant. 'I can't tell you whether Sarah will learn to talk,' she answered. 'No one can. A lot will depend on how much *you* are prepared to put in. We'll just have to wait and see how she develops. It will take a long time. Hearing children listen for many months before they say their first word. If you do these sessions at home and talk as much as possible, then you will be giving her the best chance she will have for learning language.' She opened her handbag and took out a package containing an ear mould. 'Have you brought Sarah's hearing-aid with you?' she asked.

I handed Sarah's hearing-aid over together with the harness I had made the week before. It had a pocket at the front to hold the hearing-aid and straps to go over Sarah's shoulders and around her chest. To keep the aid in place I had sewn on a button and a small piece of elastic to loop round it.

'It may take Sarah a little time to get used to wearing an ear mould so if she objects don't force her,' the teacher said as she slipped the harness over Sarah's head. 'Let her wear it for a few minutes each day and build it up until she's wearing it all the time. It will become as routine for her to put on the aid in the morning as it is to put on her vest.'

I thought of the fight I had with Sarah each morning to put on a vest and marvelled at the way the teacher made it sound so easy.

'When you speak, your voice will go into the receiver here at the top of the aid and be amplified. Look I'll show you.' The teacher told Sarah to bend her head on one side while she pushed the ear mould gently into her ear, then she switched the aid on and turned the volume control to number three. At that point a whistle blasted from the earpiece.

'When this happens you'll have to turn the hearing-aid lower,' the teacher said, as she adjusted the control. 'Sound escapes from the ear mould if it doesn't fit tightly enough and then you'll get a whistle.'

Sarah started shaking her head from side to side, disliking the feel of a strange object in her ear.

The teacher quickly removed it. 'Don't make a big thing of the aid,' she advised. 'Get her used to it slowly.'

She stood up to indicate that the lesson was at an end, and I began to gather the kind of paraphernalia which would accompany us from now on. The ear mould and the lead, the hearing-aid and the batteries, the auditory training unit, and the box with the borrowed merry-go-round in, then I thanked her.

As we walked from the building, I considered the job I had been given to do. It was my responsibility to help Sarah to speak. To speak when she had never heard the sound of her own voice, had never heard my voice either. I was unprepared and felt totally incapable of carrying out such an undertaking. Yet Sarah depended upon me.

While we were at the clinic I had left Joanne with my friend Pauline and, after I had picked her up, I raced home to try the hearing-aid on Sarah. I had a desperate need to see if she could hear and couldn't wait a moment longer.

At home I placed the harness over Sarah's shoulders . . . and removed it when she began to scream. I was determined to do this thing properly even if it did require waiting. I wasn't going to give

Sarah the chance to think the hearing-aid was important to me, no matter what it cost to curb my impatience.

When lunch was over, I carried Joanne upstairs to her cot, then returned to the kitchen. I lifted Sarah on to a chair by the table and placed the merry-go-round on the floor before sitting opposite her to begin the lesson.

'Sarah,' I said clearly. 'Here's a horse.' I raised the horse to my mouth. 'It's got a *nose*.' I touched my nose and then Sarah's. She spat at me, stood up on her chair, leaned over the table, and snatched the horse from me. When I moved to take it from her, she screamed and threw the horse across the room.

Disheartened, I pulled another piece of the merry-go-round from the box and held it to my mouth. Sarah began kicking and stamping her feet. And that was it. The lesson was over.

I picked the toy up and put it back in the box. Only then, when it was out of sight, did Sarah stop her awful screaming. Her actions seemed to say, 'I'll work with the teacher but I'm damned sure I'll not do homework as well!'

And once Sarah had made up her mind about anything, *nothing* would change it.

I went upstairs to Joanne and lay my head against her warm cheek. She reached out her hand to stroke my hair. 'Aaah,' she said. Her tiny face was framed by soft brown curls and she was smiling impishly. I loved the way she loved me.

When Mick returned from work, I strapped the aid to Sarah's chest while she played with a new toy. Mick went behind her and called her name. When she didn't turn he said, 'Perhaps she's busy concentrating on the toy. I'll try again. 'Sarah . . . SARAH. SARAH. SARAH!'

The disappointment was intense. All our hopes had been pinned on this moment. The aid was useless. Its presence now seemed to take Sarah further away from us, erecting a barrier which had not been there before. With the aid strapped to her chest we could no longer pretend she wasn't deaf.

Mick took off his jacket and sat down. 'I don't see why she can't wear it under her dress,' he said.

'The teacher told me not to put it under her clothing. She says we shouldn't try to hide it.'

I had wanted to hide the aid. It was a symbol of deafness, and deafness carried a stigma. I didn't want to feel this way but I couldn't dismiss the attitude of society just like that, one which had passed through generations, and one I had been a party to myself.

All the beliefs that society ever harboured about deafness were now turned against me: that deaf people were unintelligent and dumb, that they signed their own language, made noises instead of speech, had anti-social habits such as pulling, prodding, gesturing, that they were a sub-culture, lacked sensitivity, and had bad table manners. I had even read that in times past deafness was so feared that those afflicted with it were thrown into the river and drowned.

While Sarah was still wearing the hearing-aid, I took her to the kitchen to try and resume the lesson. It scared me to face her again. What if she wouldn't co-operate?

I put the cardboard box on the floor by the chair and Sarah ran to the closed door. When I held out my hand for her to take, she shook her head and whined, so I picked her up and sat her firmly on the chair. Then, while she scowled at me, dreadful word-less thoughts revolving in her head, I undid my wrist-watch and laid it on the table. Ten minutes. The teacher said only ten minutes.

'This is the *swing* Sarah,' I said. 'Put the *man* on the swing.' I motioned for her to do it, but she grabbed the man from my hand and refused to put him on the swing. I resisted the urge to shout, 'DO AS YOU'RE TOLD. PUT THE MAN ON THE SWING.' Instead I reached into the box for the merry-go-round top, and spun it on the table.

Sarah held my eyes with her own as she swept the merry-go-round top, still spinning, to the floor.

Each morning I brought the aid to Sarah, and each morning she refused to put it on, until the day Joanne picked up the ear mould and made an uncoordinated attempt to put it in her own ear. Seeing this, Sarah grabbed the aid and banged herself on the chest with her fist.

'Yes, it's your hearing-aid,' I said. 'You put it on then.' I motioned to her to put the harness over her head and, to my amazement, she nodded. I quickly put the aid on, fitted the ear mould in her ear, and sat her at the table. I poured cereal into a bowl and, with my heart beating furiously, I brought the merry-go-round out again.

By the time we left the table, I was walking on air. Sarah had eaten cereal and two slices of toast, she had jam on her face, and biscuit was floating in her tea – but she had put the man on the swing.

Even so when I saw the teacher again I was saying, 'I can't do it. Sarah won't listen to me.'

I didn't mention the violent feelings I was experiencing. One side of me was sympathetic towards Sarah, and the other, quite the most dominant, could literally have killed her.

'Yes you can,' the teacher replied. 'It gets easier.'

'But I'm lazy. I don't want to do it.' I was ashamed but it was true. I wanted to be free again as before, not chained to this dreadful ritual.

When we left the teacher gave us a new toy. Once we were home, I took the aeroplane out of the box while Sarah sneered at me from the other end of the table.

'The aeroplane has *wings*.' The teacher had said to use the word 'aeroplane' instead of 'plane' because longer words were easier to lipread. I had tried saying them both in front of the mirror and found them equally difficult to decipher. How Sarah was supposed to lipread when she didn't know what words meant astounded me. Besides, many letters of the alphabet didn't even appear on the lips so how could she lipread sounds which weren't visible?

Sarah continued to eye me with disdain as her foot tapped rhythmically against the window seat.

'Stop that Sarah. It has *windows*. There are the *windows*. Look, we've got some *windows* in our house.'

Sarah smacked her leg. One smack after the other.

'Keep still!' How could she see the fleeting movements of my lips if she kept fidgeting? 'The man's got a moustache.'

Sarah stared at me. Straight through me. Her look was one of defiance even though I knew that couldn't be. Sarah could only defy words when she knew they existed. A word, as far as she was concerned, may have been the way my eyebrows moved, or the number of times that I blinked.

I left the table, and even though I knew the teacher would greatly disapprove, I began to blackmail Sarah. I gave her the biggest, chewiest lollipop I had been able to buy. She looked at it, pondered upon this unexpected move, and made her decision. She put the lollipop in her mouth and raised her eyes to mine. Silently, we reached a compromise. She would do her ten minutes.

The next lesson was accompanied by another lollipop and, as I tripped over my tongue in an effort to get as many words into Sarah as I could before the lollipop disappeared, Sarah began sucking at an equally fast rate until, triumphantly, she held the lollipop stick aloft and got down from the table. I looked at my watch in dismay. Five minutes. Only five minutes.

So it was a battle of wits between Sarah and me. The only thing was, she was winning!

3.   *And the water ran silently*

Towards the end of October Sarah wore her hearing-aid for the first time outside the house. I had come this way with Sarah and Joanne many times in the last five weeks, but today there was a new kind of pain. The aid was tangible evidence of Sarah's deafness: there for all the world to see.

The aid lay in the harness beneath Sarah's coat, but the lead and ear mould were visible still. As Sarah moved, the coat rubbed against the microphone. It sounded like the scratching of sand-paper, only Sarah didn't notice.

We had almost reached the shops when Sarah started to take off her coat and I reached forward to stop her. Then the words, 'Her acceptance will depend upon yours,' flashed across my mind. I took my hand away.

While I struggled for the need for a new kind of acceptance, someone called my name. I turned round, and Sarah ran into the road in front of a large red bus. I chased after her, and the pushchair with Joanne inside rolled down the incline behind me.

I pulled Sarah, and the pushchair, back up the slope and heard my neighbour say loudly, 'I was just telling . . .' she indicated her companion, 'that you have to run after Sarah because she's deaf and can't hear you call.'

I stood still, her voice ringing in my ears. She couldn't know of the hurt in that one small word. By using it she made Sarah different. Sarah wasn't any different, she had always been the same, only now she had a label, and the label divided.

My sense of isolation increased. I was utterly and totally alone. I had nothing in common with any other mother here. They knew what they were doing and where they were going with their children. Everything that was normal in their 'hearing' child's day was a deprivation for Sarah. Having breakfast, playing, putting on shoes, watching the television, looking at a book . . . were as nothing without the sound of my voice to share it with her. This wasn't *a* tragedy, but a *continuing* tragedy, for 'deafness' lay in the everyday occurrences. This meant that no one, neither relative nor friend, had the opportunity to understand the real meaning of deafness to Sarah. Yet I needed their understanding.

I went to the supermarket where I pushed Sarah and Joanne around in a trolley. I had to keep Sarah close to me always in case she ran out of the door. She had no sense whatever of danger.

Halfway down the shopping aisle we passed the shelves of sweets and Sarah reached out and whined.

'No Sarah,' I said, 'it's dinner-time soon. No.' I shook my head firmly so she couldn't mistake my meaning and waggled my finger, which made Joanne giggle.

Sarah clenched her fists, arched her back over the side of the trolley, and her violent scream rent the air. If only I could make her understand what 'dinner-time' meant. It didn't seem fair to expect her to accept 'no' without an explanation.

People turned at Sarah's scream. I hurriedly motioned 'eating food' then held up my finger to indicate she must wait. She opened her mouth to scream again . . . and I gave her the sweets.

I imagined everyone thinking what a horrid spoiled child she was, because that's how she sounded, but when they noticed the aid their expressions changed, and that was even worse.

Near to tears, I bundled my groceries into carrier-bags and left the shop. Outside, I strapped Joanne into the pushchair and forcibly removed Sarah from a small boy's bike. She screamed and kicked out with her feet, not realizing that the toy had an owner, and it wasn't her. In our struggle the shopping spilt on to the pavement. A man helped me to retrieve it.

Sarah's aid was whistling incessantly as she sat moodily beside Joanne in the pushchair and when we were almost home she began to scream. I picked her up and, holding a carrier-bag in each hand, propelled the pushchair forward with my stomach. When I found I couldn't steer it properly I said to Sarah: 'It's no good you'll have to walk.' I bent to release her but she clung frantically to my neck, screaming and kicking and gesturing for me to drop the bags instead. I was trying to pull her hands free when a lady, who had been watching Sarah's performance, walked out of a shop and strode purposefully towards us.

'Whatever is the matter with that child?' she demanded, and, without waiting for a reply, she took Sarah from my arms and plonked her unceremoniously on to the pavement. Sarah was so shocked by this treatment her screams died.

The lady was trying to help me so I felt I owed her an explanation. There was a lump in my throat as I said, 'Sarah's deaf,' before turning to walk away. I carried the bags, and pushed the pushchair, and Sarah quietly followed.

It was the first time I had ever used the word 'deaf' and the last time I made deafness an excuse for bad behaviour.

Perhaps it was because I was so unsure of how to treat Sarah that I received advice from every quarter, from people who had no experience of deafness whatever. 'Be patient,' some said, 'she doesn't understand,' while others longed for me to smack her.

I read that I mustn't feel pity, that pity was a destructive emotion. Each time I thought I may be pitying Sarah I sang aloud to erase the word from my head. When I thought that no matter how long I lived I would never get used to Sarah being deaf, I felt guilty. Was that pity?

In between these bouts of intense grief I was detached and empty. I wondered if I lacked compassion for surely it was sad.

At the end of October I met Lucy. She was five years old, she was deaf, and she went to an ordinary school.

'Where's Lucy's hearing-aid?' I asked her mother.

'It's here,' she replied, and she lifted Lucy's long brown hair to show me.

There was an ear mould like Sarah's, but what was different was the tiny hearing-aid which fitted neatly behind Lucy's ear. Sarah's body-aid was almost four times the size.

'Lucy's just recited a nursery rhyme at school for the Harvest Festival,' said her mother. 'Afterwards everyone was so kind and they congratulated me on how well she was doing.'

'That's marvellous,' I said, really pleased for her. 'Do you think Lucy would say it for me?'

Lucy was persuaded to leave her game and reluctantly she began to sing 'Baa Baa Black Sheep' for me. She stood in the middle of the room with her hands clasped tightly behind her back and as I strained to hear her quiet words, a feeling of elation began to grow in me. I understood her.

Lucy could speak.

Her voice was not like the boy's in the waiting-room: she had an impediment but oh it was ever so slight. I could barely contain my feelings. Lucy and her nursery rhyme had given me hope. She had also given me something to work towards.

I had a goal at last!

'It's fantastic,' I said. 'What did you do with her?' I was aware now, more than ever before, that my ignorance was a barrier to Sarah.

'We had a teacher come to the house and he showed me how to train Lucy's hearing. He called it auditory training and I had to make –' Lucy's mother stopped in mid-sentence. Sarah had slapped Lucy across the face and was tearing at her hair.

'I'm so sorry,' I said, dragging Sarah away by the legs.

'What else did I do?' Lucy's mother murmured after Lucy had stopped crying. 'I let Lucy hear the different sounds in the house. The vacuum-cleaner, the washing-machine, you know.'

'Sarah wouldn't be able to hear those sounds.'

'I would have thought if Sarah's been given a hearing-aid it must mean she's got some hearing which can be trained.'

We talked for an hour or more and by the time Lucy and her mother had left the house I had lots of ideas to work on. She was right. If Sarah was totally deaf she wouldn't have been given a hearing-aid. Excitement ran through me. Today was the day Sarah was going to discover sound.

I could hardly wait to get the auditory training unit out from behind the settee and with Sarah and Joanne trailing behind me, I carried it to the bathroom. I put the auditory training unit on the floor and the earphones on Sarah's head. Sarah stood with her body rigid, rejecting them, and me, for imposing them upon her. I turned the taps on in the bath and held the microphone to the gushing water, before pointing to my ear.

'Sarah you must *listen*.' I held my head on one side, frowned to show the concentration that was needed, and pointed to my ear again. *'Listen.'*

Sarah did try. She stood still, and she listened – and my heart ached for her.

I didn't know whether it was my imagination but I seemed to detect from the expression in her eyes that a ripple of sound had crossed over the barrier of her deafness. When I looked closer though, there was no indication she had heard the water at all. And so the moment for discovering sound passed.

Despondently I removed the earphones, and damp curls clustered around Sarah's head from their pressure. I placed the earphones on Joanne to include her too, and with her head on one side, her face still with concentration, I saw in her green eyes what I had so longed to see in Sarah's. She clapped her hands, excitedly

nodding her head, as if to say this was the very first time she had
heard the sound of running water.

'Joanne, you big actress.' I swung her into my arms, then
kneeling bent down to cuddle Sarah. But she pushed me away and
pinched my cheeks until they hurt.

Sarah wore her earphones as we went from room to room
banging doors, rattling keys, clapping hands. In the kitchen I held
the microphone near the washing-machine as the water swished
against the glass door. I switched on the radio and the television
too but it wasn't until we reached the vacuum-cleaner that I knew
for certain Sarah *could* hear. She lay her head against the cylinder
as the engine sounded and concentrated hard. She didn't blink.
Her eyes didn't widen. But her look had changed.

It held recognition.

I stood, trying to capture the moment for ever.

Then I saw the truth. Sarah *had* heard the sound of the water
running from the taps in the bath, she just hadn't connected the
sound with the water.

The water had always run silently before.

Now I knew what I had to do. I had to give sound meaning. Like
a newborn baby, Sarah would have to *recognize* every sound around
her too.

It would take time for Sarah to associate the 'whirring' noise
with the washing-machine, and the 'bang' with the door. She
would have to learn the sound each one made before she could
recognize they were different from each other.

As with a hearing child, there were many thousands of sounds to
learn and to discriminate between for instant recall. The more
sounds Sarah could be introduced to, the wider her knowledge of
the environment would grow. In this way her hearing *would*
improve because it would be able to identify more and more
sounds.

I told Mick about the breakthrough Sarah had made and though
he thought it incredible, he couldn't see how it had been possible.

I tried explaining that, while she wouldn't hear the vacuum-
cleaner in the same way we hear it (because she couldn't hear all
the pitches within the sound), she could still come to recognize the
sound *she heard* as the vacuum-cleaner.

And so, while I moved towards a greater involvement with
Sarah, and a deeper insight into her problems, Mick had yet to
discover that something *could* be done. Perhaps this was when he

first started to feel apart from us, or it may have been even earlier. Sarah had demanded my time from the day she was born.

'Mick, I'm going to teach Sarah to talk like Lucy,' I said. I was still in a triumphant frame of mind. 'I've got to do it before she's five and goes to school. Lucy's mother says that's very important.' I didn't say I wanted Sarah to go to an ordinary school. But that was my aim.

As we talked, I began cutting out pictures of objects and pasting them on to cardboard as Lucy's mother had shown me how to do, then writing words beneath like: 'This is the *watch*.' 'Here is a *pencil*.' 'This is a *camel*.' I found a photograph of Sarah and wrote her name below in large letters. Tomorrow Sarah was going to learn her name. She was nearly three. It was a long time to be a nobody.

In the morning I hurriedly dressed Sarah and, after switching on her aid, I knelt before her on the kitchen floor.

'Sarah,' I said, as I held the photo to my mouth. 'This is you.' I pointed first to the photograph and then to her. *'Sarah.'*

Sarah snatched the photo from me and held it possessively to her chest as if to say, 'It's me. This is mine.'

I took it from her and held it to my mouth again. 'Sarah. You're *Sarah.'*

Sarah knew I had spoken but she didn't know she had a name, so I repeated 'Sarah, you're *Sarah*' over and over again.

During breakfast, inspiration dawned. I took Sarah by the hand to the mirror in the hall. She couldn't mistake my meaning now. 'You're *Sarah*,' I said, as I pointed first to her image in the mirror, then to the photograph, and finally to herself. *'Sarah.'*

Sarah nodded, patiently humouring my obsession.

All morning I thought deeply about it. Why didn't Sarah recognize her name? I couldn't make my meaning clearer. It was almost as if she was slow. By dinner-time I had the answer.

The name 'Sarah' was totally without relevance *because no one else had a name either*!

I delved once more into the box of photographs and selected two. Beneath one I wrote '*Joanne*', beneath the other, '*Mummy and Daddy*'.

With Sarah and Joanne sitting at the table, I held Joanne's baby photo aloft. 'This is *Joanne*,' I said. I pointed first to the photo and then to Joanne. 'Joanne,' I repeated.

I held up the next photo. 'This is *Daddy*. I'm *Mummy*.'

Sarah stopped eating, her spoon suspended in mid-air. She pointed to Joanne.

'That's *Joanne*,' I said.

She pointed to me.

'I'm *Mummy*.'

She pointed again and squealed.

'That's *Daddy*.'

Her hand banged her chest.

'Sarah.'

It was as if a whole new world had opened up for Sarah, enlarging the confines of her mind. All afternoon her insisting finger pointed to photographs as one by one relatives and friends tumbled into existence. When we went to the shops her finger continued with poignant determination as lady, man, Peter, baby, and John, answered the great need within her. Sarah had been brought firmly into our midst.

Sarah was somebody.

4.   *The continuous droning*

I went to see the teacher with my 'goal' in mind. Enthusiastically, I repeated my aim to her but instead of sharing my exhilaration, she frowned.

'Mrs Robinson, you mustn't compare Sarah with Lucy. Sarah's hearing loss is much more severe than Lucy's.' Then she tried to soften the blow. 'No child should be compared with another, they're all different and they achieve different things.'

From that moment on, I wanted to get away from her. Her words had crystallized all I had ever feared about deafness. She was saying I should set my sights lower. That Sarah was one of those children for whom the effects of deafness could not be overcome.

It was my introduction to the great divide. Not all children were equally deaf. It just wasn't fair. It appeared that from a wide range of impairment – the hard of hearing, the partially hearing, the severely and the profoundly deaf – we must accept an equally wide range of attainment.

Perhaps Sarah would never talk to me. She couldn't hear her own voice. She had missed listening for eight hundred and seventy days, thousands of lost hours. She had missed our voices from the day she was born. I wanted so much to know her. Now would I ever? She might never buy a sweet in a shop, have a friend, read or write.

But what if I learned quickly? Could I change the direction in which Sarah was heading? I had only two years to do what usually took five – and Sarah was deaf. Instead of expanding her language as I would a hearing child's of the same age, I would begin at the beginning. Sarah and I would start together.

The next morning, after we had waved goodbye to Mick, I laid the picture cards I had made on the floor with a chocolate Smartie beside each one. When I was ready, I called loudly to Sarah, then, as she didn't turn, I stamped on the floor, and this made her spin round immediately.

In time Sarah would come to recognize her name but she would have to have *heard* it repeated many times before she would realize that the vague two-syllabled sound – 'Eh-ah' – meant her.

The picture cards were a new game so Sarah decided to join me. She let me put the earphones on her head, providing Joanne moved away from my side (this she indicated by a dismissive wave), and waited for the game to begin.

'This is the *pig*,' I said, holding the picture to my mouth. '*Pig*,' I repeated, before handing the microphone to Sarah hoping she would say something too.

'Pi,' she repeated, blowing the sound explosively from between her lips, and pointing to the picture.

Joanne clapped her hands. I rejoiced. And Sarah, well, she ate the Smartie! I thought she was the cleverest little girl that had ever lived. She knew the pattern on my lips meant the animal in the picture, and that the animal in the picture was a 'pi'.

Within a few days Sarah could say ten words. She had realized there were names for all things, both living and dead; *I* had realized how names made our surroundings coherent to us. They were a simple and ingenious, cataloguing system.

Now Sarah had a vocabulary it was possible to begin training her hearing so that eventually she might recognize the forty sounds which make up speech and the almost infinite number of words which can be formed from them. But, for the moment, all I wanted Sarah to do was to recognize the differences between the ten words, so she would know that 'pig' was not the same as 'camel' and 'dog' not the same as 'watch'.

It had taken me ages to understand this because as a hearing person, the differences were obvious to me. Sarah hadn't a clear auditory image of words though, and all sound appeared very much the same to her. 'Hearing' babies react to sound from the day they are born. They begin noting fractional differences between sounds. In time they note differences between words. Before long they recognize words.

About two weeks after I had first introduced the picture cards, I began helping Sarah to become aware of those differences. I scattered the cards on the floor and went behind her to say into the microphone, 'Give me the *camel*.'

Sarah ran behind a chair.

What could I do? I had the microphone switched on, the controls on the auditory training unit set, the cards ready, and Sarah wouldn't play. I knew she was testing me. She must have sensed how much I wanted her to listen.

'Joanne would you like to play?' I asked, beckoning her to me.

Joanne shuffled across the room on her bottom to kneel before me, her white frilly pants on show.

'Give me the watch,' I said, very loudly into the microphone in the hope Sarah might hear me as well.

Joanne passed the picture, and I made a great fuss of her as she picked up the Smartie and put it in her pinafore pocket, no doubt to be offered to Sarah later.

Sarah watched from her position behind the chair, her face contorted with jealousy. She didn't want my attention, she didn't want the Smartie, but she *did* want Joanne removed from the limelight.

It was Sarah's jealousy of Joanne which brought her into our midst. We could have lost her, and we nearly did. Many deaf children withdraw from a world they find perplexing and difficult, but Sarah was a fighter and that saved her.

Joanne willingly moved to one side to let Sarah take her place, then pointed to her ear to explain to Sarah that she must listen because if she did, she would get a Smartie.

Sarah snarled, and I felt sad that Joanne rarely received any other kind of communication from Sarah. Not that Joanne seemed to notice, she continued blithely in her own sweet way.

'Give me the *pig*.'

Sarah scanned the cards, and her hand moved slowly over each until she decided which picture the short explosive sound belong to. When she picked up the 'pig' Joanne nodded her head approvingly.

'Give me the *camel*.'

Sarah's reaction was quicker this time. There were only two cards on the floor containing two-syllabled sounds and 'camel' was higher in pitch and rhythmically different to the snappier sound of 'watch'. I was deeply impressed that Sarah could play the game at all. She had to work out from the smallest amount of evidence, minute differences in the length, intonation and rhythmical pattern of words, when they were but a blurred distortion of sounds all rolled into one.

'Give me the *cat* Sarah.'

Joanne's finger peeped from beneath the folds of her dress and pointed in the direction of the cat, and Sarah, ignoring her, passed me the 'dog' instead. It was her way of informing me she had decided to call a halt to the game. I quickly intervened with: 'Good girl Sarah. I think we'll finish now.'

This pitting of wits was extraordinary. It was almost as if Sarah was able to manipulate a great many thoughts, yet this belied her age and experience. Her calculations were sophisticated, and, to keep one step ahead of her, my ingenuity was stretched in a way it had never needed to be stretched before.

'Sarah we're going to *Pauline*'s house.'

'Paua,' Sarah repeated, and I loved her for trying.

She could copy any words I said but that is not what language is about. Language is to do with deriving meaning from words.

'We're going to Pauline's,' I said again in despair. Pauline. What was Pauline? Pauline was a movement of the lips, not a person, not a friend. I got a pencil and drew a car and a house. Sarah turned away from me.

'We're going in the car Sarah.' I mimed driving. She shook her head.

I clenched my fists in frustration. If she knew where we were going she would have come straightaway. I pointed to the window for her to see the car outside, and moved to lift her into my arms. She quickly grasped the door knob and when I pulled her fingers away, she put them back. I prized her hand from the knob. The other hand took its place.

Sarah screamed as I caught hold of her wrists and pulled her from the room, then dragged her through the kitchen while she tried to grasp everything within reach, doors, chairs, table legs. Finally, I carried her to the car, and though she was screaming her head off and tearing at my hair, I strapped her in.

I then carried Joanne to the car, started the engine, and drove to Pauline's while Sarah kept up her frenzied attacks on me all the way. I was torn by ambivalent feelings. She was deaf. I wanted to love and protect her. I also wanted to smack her very hard.

Through the rear-view mirror I could see Joanne smiling at Sarah's hysterics and wondered how she could remain so un-affected by it all.

As we turned the corner near Pauline's house the pitch in Sarah's screams changed as she realized where we were going. Now they held a proud, defiant note. I stopped the car, and when

Sarah refused to get out, I carried Joanne to the front door of the house.

Pauline and I were standing in the kitchen talking when Sarah pushed open the door. She saw us looking down the hallway towards her and, holding her head high, she put her hands on her hips. She stood, a defiant figure, silhouetted against the bevelled glass.

'You deserve a good smack Sarah.' I held up my hand, and she looked me squarely in the eye.

'Just look,' said Pauline. 'I've never seen such defiance. She couldn't care less whether you smack her or not.'

At that all pretence left me. 'But what shall I do Pauline? How shall I treat her?'

It was the first time I had asked for advice or admitted I couldn't cope. Pauline never seemed to have problems with her children, and she had four. I was the one who experienced difficulties. It must be something I was doing.

'What do you mean?' Pauline said. 'Surely you would treat her normally, she's a normal child.'

I changed the subject in a fit of pique. Pauline obviously thought I could treat Sarah as a hearing child. 'We've been playing this game at home,' I said, 'where Sarah has to pass me picture cards using her hearing alone. Would you like to see it? . . .'

'What can Sarah hear exactly?' Pauline asked as the game ended. 'When you said, "Give me the camel," what would she have heard?'

'The low-pitched sounds: something like "I ee a aa-u."'

'So that's why deaf children speak the way they do.' Pauline shook her head. 'I hadn't thought of it before.'

'Sarah's supposed to compensate by lipreading. On lipreading alone "Give me the camel" will look something like "Iv m th m-l".'

'What are these games for?' Pauline lifted Joanne on to her knee; Joanne lay back and sucked her thumb.

'They're to help train Sarah's hearing. She's got to learn to listen.'

'Wouldn't it help if you turned the hearing-aid louder?'

'If I do that the distortion is amplified too. If Sarah hears "Give me the camel" as "I ee a aa-u" then louder it will be "I EE A AA-U."'

I was grateful to Pauline for listening to me. Trying to explain it to her helped to unravel the muddle in my mind. Her son Christopher had been born the same day as Sarah and in the same nursing home. Pauline and I hadn't known then how different would be the paths Sarah and Christopher would follow. The late diagnosis of Sarah's deafness had made her handicap a million times worse than it need ever have been.

'How Mick?' Pauline asked. 'I haven't seen him for a while.'

'I think he's trying to shut everything out of his mind.'

Mick seemed to have accepted Sarah's deafness but not how it was changing our lives. When Sarah had screamed at breakfast this morning he had shouted, 'Why can't we be normal like everyone else?' He saw our friends leading carefree lives while ours seemed to revolve around lessons, tantrums and rows.

I wished Mick could talk to someone.

When we left I had a bag of toys which Pauline had lent me to use in the lessons. On our way home we passed a horse in a field and, seeing it there, sparked off an idea. Sarah had been given a lovely wooden farm but she wouldn't play with it. Not once had she picked up the toy horse and said 'ore' even though she knew its name. I reversed up to the gate to have a clearer view of the horse.

'That's a *horse* Sarah,' I said, turning to face her. Then I rummaged through the toys until I found what I was looking for. 'This is a *horse* too.' I held up the toy. 'They're both *horses*. That one there and this one here. *Horses*.'

Sarah looked at the toy in my hand and she looked at the horse in the field. I repeated my words and she stared fixedly at my mouth.

Then understanding began to dawn on her face. It was as if a light shone where no light had shone before – and I knew something wondrous was happening.

Sarah pointed to both horses in turn. 'Ore,' she said.

At last I understood. Sarah hadn't associated the toy horse with a real horse before. As far as she knew the horse in the field had a different name. How could she have known one was a replica of the other if no one had told her before?

Now I knew why Sarah hadn't wanted to play with the farm, or the roundabout, or the aeroplane. She couldn't possibly re-enact in a game what was not reality for her.

And perhaps there is no reality without words.

Sarah would have to learn from life before representations of it would have meaning. Tomorrow we would go and visit a farm and I would take our toy farmyard with us.

At home Pauline's words, 'Treat her normally, she's a normal child,' refused to leave me. Sarah *was* different, but was she different because she was deaf? Before we had known about her deafness she hadn't behaved as badly as she did now – and yet *she had always been deaf.* It was Sarah's behaviour which had changed, and in allowing this behaviour *we were making her different.*

It was a sobering conclusion to draw. I loved Sarah but what about when she was older? No one would tolerate her behaviour as we did, and she was getting worse with each day that passed. Our responsibility was to help Sarah become an acceptable person, both to herself and to others, particularly as she was deaf.

Once again I was torn between an inclination to indulge her and the knowledge that she must be disciplined to develop. But Sarah could not hear normally, and she could not speak normally. What right had we to expect normality in these circumstances?

I worried about it all afternoon. By seven o'clock I had decided that, instead of making allowances for Sarah, I would treat her as any other three-year-old, although I would always respect that fact that she couldn't hear. Sarah was bright. Even if she couldn't understand the reasons for doing certain things, she knew when I approved and when I did not. From now on I was going to be really patient in trying to make her understand but, if that failed, she would have to learn to accept a plain 'yes' or 'no'.

Light-headed with relief, I went to look for Sarah and found her in the lounge emptying the contents of my purse down the back of the settee.

'No Sarah,' I said firmly. 'Put the money back in the purse please.'

Sarah saw my words and actions. She lifted her arms and with all the force she could muster, threw a coin at the window. When Mick heard the sound, almost like a gun firing, he came running into the room to see a crack extending from one end of the window to the other.

He stood unable to speak, and I moved in front of Sarah to hide the smile which was spreading over her face.

'I think it's time they went to bed,' Mick said at last.

He picked Joanne up to take her upstairs and I held Sarah's nightie out to her. 'Sarah put your nightie on please.'

She stiffened.

'Come on Sarah.'

Her hands went to her hips. Her foot tapped the floor.

I moved to undress her and she began to cry. Not an ordinary cry. It was without emotion. Without tears.

Sarah was exceptionally strong for her age and the struggle was undignified. I held her rigid body between my knees, contained a flaying arm, dodged punches and kicks, and, prizing her fingers from the cuff of her sweater, I forced her stiffened arm from the sleeve.

'Take your socks off now.'

I touched her ankle, she caught my face with her hand.

'Sarah if you take one sock off, I'll take the other one off for you.'

I mimed my intentions; she shook her head and ran away screeching like some injured creature. I smacked her leg. Hard. She stood before me defiantly shrugging her shoulders.

'Take off your socks,' I shouted. 'Other children go to bed. You've got to do the same as other children.'

Sarah howled as she bent to take her sock from her foot, then threw it at me.

'Now the other one.'

She ran round the furniture. I ran after her. I chased her round and round until, suddenly, Sarah stopped. She stood with her hands on her hips daring me to touch her. I smacked her leg and took the sock from her foot. She ran to the table and hysterically swept the books to the floor.

It seemed like hours later that Mick brought Joanne in to say goodnight. Her cheeks were pink from her bath and she smelled of talcum powder. I held out my arms and she fell towards me gurgling happily. I looked at Sarah. Her face was flushed, her eyes swollen with crying. Why wouldn't she get undressed?

Mick took Joanne upstairs and I turned to Sarah again. She was spent and I was almost beaten. If I gave in now she would fight even harder against going to bed tomorrow night. I held out one of her slippers, and she curled her toes.

'PUT YOUR FOOT IN.'

Sarah put her foot half in and half out of the slipper.

I pretended I hadn't seen this. I didn't want to break her spirit. She would need it someday. Probably to break me.

Mick came in. 'This has gone on long enough,' he said. 'Come on Sarah, up you come.' He swung her into his arms and though she fought to get down, he carried her to bed.

We had learned, if Sarah wasn't to wander the house all evening, to close her bedroom door, so, after we had looked at some pictures in a book and kissed her goodnight, we did just that.

Sarah started screaming and banging on the door. She pulled at the door knob and kicked. She howled. She screamed.

'If we go into her she'll think we're weakening and go on all the more,' I said. Although every instinct within me wanted to go to her, I knew I should not. Sarah had ruled the roost too long.

In the end, she began pacing the floor like a caged lion. Then the pacing stopped. She sat on the floor, as she always did, cross-legged, and struck her head repeatedly against the wall.

Bang. Bang. Bang.

It was almost as if she was trying to drive something away.

What that something was, Sarah was to keep secret for another seven years.

Throughout the evening Mick and I took it in turns to listen outside her door and, at about eleven o'clock, when she could no longer resist sleep, she curled up on the floor behind the door sucking her finger. As she sucked, a continuous droning sound came from her throat.

When that stopped Mick opened the door and lifted her into bed.

5.   *A jigsaw-puzzle world*

'Sarah eat your toast *quickly*,' I said, and made fast chewing movements to indicate what I meant.

A new teacher of the deaf was coming to visit us this morning and I wanted to find time to bring a semblance of order to the house.

'Gagon.' Sarah spread the palms of her hands and shrugged her shoulders.

'No, it hasn't *all gone*.' My heart quickened. It was Sarah's joke, pretending she couldn't see the toast on her plate. 'Here it is.'

'Poppi.'

'Don't tell me to *stop it*.'

'Goaa.' Sarah pointed.

'It's not *Joanne's* toast. It's your *toast*.' My ears tingled at the sound of Sarah's voice. Her proper voice.

Our exchange, Sarah's and mine, made me want to sing out loud for it was only on rare occasions she actually offered words to me. These spontaneous utterances were worth a million repeated ones of mine, and I treasured each as one would the most precious pearl.

At ten o'clock the teacher arrived. Miss Ayling was about fifty, she had short grey hair, and an impeccably neat appearance. She would come every Monday from now on.

'Hello Sarah.' Miss Ayling smiled broadly at Sarah. 'I'm *shutting* the door.' She shut the door and held up her car keys. 'Here are my *keys*.'

The words were perfectly formed on her lips and, as Sarah's eyes moved momentarily to the keys, Miss Ayling waited. When they returned to her, she continued, 'I'll put them in my *handbag*.' She placed the keys in her handbag. 'You *shut* the handbag.'

As Miss Ayling spoke, she gestured her words. Sarah shut the handbag then waited expectantly for the next instruction, her face serious and attentive.

They went into the lounge together and I followed carrying

Joanne on my hip. Usually she was a noisy child, always cooing, or gurgling, or squealing with delight, but now she was listening carefully to Miss Ayling and gaining as much, if not more, than Sarah.

Lately I had found myself testing her hearing with ever-increasing frequency. I clapped my hands behind her back, knocked on doors, and dropped keys, in the same way I had once for Sarah. But I couldn't seem to separate 'deafness' from 'hearing' in my mind. I couldn't decide whether she was responding to some stimulus other than sound. I heard Miss Ayling saying to Sarah, '*Sit down*. Sit *beside* me.' She patted a cushion and Sarah obligingly sat down, her gaze never moving from Miss Ayling's face, her hands folded on her knee.

'You're sitting *beside* me,' Miss Ayling continued, and she patted Sarah's thigh, then her own. 'Look. Here's my *purse*. It's *open*.' Miss Ayling motioned an opening gesture with her hands. '*Shut* the purse.' She brought the palms of her hands together. Sarah shut the purse.

'Udder purder,' she said.

'Good girl. *You shut* the purse.' Miss Ayling pointed to Sarah and Sarah nodded. She knew what she had done. She had *shut* the purse.

They moved into the dining-room and I followed with a burgeoning sense of gratitude. Miss Ayling was combining words with actions and Sarah couldn't fail to understand. That was what communication was: making another person understand. Sarah was actively involved in the *meaning* of words.

More than this, Sarah was gaining from two people. Now the burden of my responsibility was shared. It was another who prompted the words which tripped readily from Sarah's lips, 'key', 'door', 'Daddy gone car', 'Grandma'.

Before the work had seemed so difficult. Now the stunning simplicity of it all was unravelled before my eyes. And it was a revelation to me.

Sarah must be taught that there are ways to describe how the door shuts, and the light goes on, the way we sit, and where we go. It wasn't just about telling her the names of all things from the floor to the sky, but communicating the world simply and easily.

I felt the joy rise up in me. I could do that.

At last I saw the extent of my responsibility towards Sarah. If she was ever to catch up she must receive a continuous stream of information for all her waking hours. As I looked around me, I saw a world which jostled to be described, a world which I must share.

Nothing had prepared me for this. I had thought I would be the mother of a hearing child, not the mother of a deaf child. I was a physical education teacher not a teacher of the deaf.

I wasn't persevering, single-minded or determined. I was selfish rather than selfless. I did have a strong will-power but this meant stubborness more than anything else. I was indolent, liked my own way, and hated routine.

'All mothers teach their children in a sense,' Miss Ayling told me as she lifted Sarah on to a chair. 'They are passing their knowledge of language, and its structure, on to their toddlers.'*

From now on, I decided, I would believe that every single word I said would be recorded in Sarah's memory, and every word I repeated would be one step nearer to Sarah understanding and then using that word.

Afterwards, Sarah participated in the lesson but with restraint. She wanted to please Miss Ayling, at least that was the impression she gave, but so tight was the control she imposed upon herself that it was impossible for her to enjoy the work. Sometimes I wondered if Sarah was capable of enjoyment. On Sunday we had gone to the park and Grandma commented, 'I've never seen a child unhappy on a swing before.'

When the lesson was over I took a deep breath and said, 'Sarah doesn't like the lessons and she hates the earphones.'

Miss Ayling took a sip of her coffee. 'Have you thought of taking the earphones into the other room?' she asked. 'You don't have to be sitting at a table to do a lesson, and you can use anything that's around the house to talk about. A tea-set, even a bunch of pegs. If you think about it, mothers talk to their children whenever the opportunity arises. We're merely trying to create that opportunity.'

That's what deafness is, I thought: a missed opportunity. It was also a handicap which grew with each passing day – one that was demeaning to all human dignity. Without language life was surely meaningless.

When Miss Ayling left I was ready to talk forever but, with the door closing, a dark mood fell upon Sarah. I ran upstairs to distract her and she and Joanne came after me.

---

* This applies to any language, and to any method or methods used in encouraging that language.

In the bedroom I placed Sarah strategically opposite me. 'We'll make the *bed*. *Pull* up the sheet. *Flatten* it.' Even as I spoke the words sounded empty. It was always the same at the beginning.

Sarah copied my actions, her expression exaggerating the effort needed. 'Bummy,' she said out of the blue.

I checked myself. Had I heard her correctly? Then, convinced, I dived on the bed shouting with happiness. Sarah had said 'Mummy'. It was so beautiful I wanted to hear it again and again.

'Geggy, geggy, go.' Sarah jumped on top of me. Joanne threw herself at my head.

'Ready, steady, go,' I repeated, swinging them both in the air. What did I care about lessons when Sarah made me feel on top of the world. This side of her was special in an undefinable way, while the other, the deaf side, was bedevilled by black moods and tension. Deafness changed Sarah. It camouflaged her true self. The difficulty was in separating the two.

'Here's a *pillow* for Joanne,' I said. I passed it to her and laughed to see her blow an indulgent 'p' before burying her head in its feathery softness, her curls shining against the white linen case. 'A pillow for you Sarah. Let's *bang* it.'

Sarah almost forgot her rigid control as she pummelled pillows energetically.

I moved towards the door and Sarah and Joanne followed. In Joanne's room we discovered yet another 'bed'. I continued, 'Pull up the *blanket, tuck* it in,' while Sarah and Joanne, exchanging conspiratorial winks, shouted, 'Geggy, geggy, go,' and amidst uproarious giggles, they burrowed under the blankets leaving my best-laid plans well and truly thwarted.

The beds weren't made that day, nor for many days to come; instead we played with beds until Sarah's 'make bed' was heard. She knew what the words stood for, she said the words, now she needed repetition to imprint them on her mind for ever. We carried on with the lesson on a small doll's cot until we were all heartily sorry that *beds* had even been invented.

Beds though, and other such objects, were never the real issue. With Sarah's spoken words, the suffocating hold which deafness had upon her was finally, and irrevocably, loosed. In these first glimmers of comprehension Sarah had taken the incalculable leap. Her first words had travelled the distance of a million years, from man's primeval beginnings, through toil, struggle and advancement, to our intelligence now.

Sarah was communicating in our culture, our world.

And I was reaching her. A real – and a different – relationship was beginning. It brought me more joy than I had a right to expect.

I sought more information about deafness. Miss Ayling had given me a reading list and I joined charities like the National Deaf Children's Society and received their valuable publications. I read about the experiences of other parents of deaf children, professional articles too, though the complexity of the language was often a barrier. Sometimes I would glean information in an arbitrary way but it was rarely encouraging. Without doubt the most chilling sentence was about learning language. It lay amongst a host of other words near a photograph of a young girl and it said:

> The optimum period for learning language is in the first three years of life.

I read on feverishly: the early years were when a child was most receptive to language, which made stimulation within that period crucial; and might not deafness lead to atrophy of the hearing system and parts of the brain concerned with language, if stimulation was not given?

But Sarah was three already! So life became serious for me. Short cuts must be taken, I must always be concise, allow nothing to be wasted. My language became vividly alive, my face more expressive, and my actions dramatic and exaggerated.

If Sarah was to have language, and one day speech, all her faculties must be used, and in a way which would not normally be expected of them. They would have to support and compensate for the incomplete image she was receiving. Without this it would be too much to expect Sarah to recall those words which could only ever be a faint or imperfectly grooved pattern in her memory.

Despite not being allowed the luxury of learning language at her own pace, Sarah's development was not so different from that of a younger, hearing, child. When she saw a fly on the window she squealed, and pointed.

'That's a *fly*,' I said.

'Iy.'

Thereafter, all things which flew were flies. Birds were flies, butterflies were flies, moths were flies, and nothing, absolutely nothing, would change Sarah's mind.

I wondered what I could do. I would have to introduce the word 'not'. But what does 'not' mean? It has no shape or substance, so how could I form a picture for her?

The next time Sarah called a bee an 'iy' I shook my head vigorously. 'It's *not* a fly. It's a *bee*.'

'Not' was a useful little word. 'It's *not*', a shake of the head, 'a bee, it's a *bird*. It's *not*', a shake of the head, 'a bird, it's a spider. It's *not*', a shake of the head, 'a spider, it's a *worm*.'

In our search for these creatures we found *dust*. Beneath the dust was *concrete*. By the side of the concrete was *earth*, and upon it a *cobweb*. We discovered the *floor* on our *knees*, and then a *table*, a *chair*, *cups, knives, jam, pickles, buttons, cheese, cotton, ink, saucepans, pens, paper, apples, spoons* . . . hundreds of objects, each to be repeated a hundred times over, in a hundred different ways. Not only could I *brush* the floor, I could *mop, wipe, clean, sweep, scrub*, or *rub* it.

Each day more was revealed. From 'not' we moved to 'like'. 'Like' meant not the same, but similar. I could say: 'It's not a horse, it's *like* a horse. It's a *donkey*.' And then: 'It's *like* a mouse. It's a *rat*.'

Working like this made me aware. Without me, Sarah's destiny was a life on the fringe, half in our world, and half not. Because I was the one who interpreted for her, I was a friend, a neighbour, an aunt, the television, sadness, and laughter. I was even Mick.

Mick had stopped talking to Sarah. He loved her, cuddled and kissed her. But he didn't speak to her. He had stopped saying 'Hiya Sarah' when he walked in the door, because he knew she wouldn't understand. When he tried saying 'Hello' as I suggested he do, the words sounded forced and unnatural. The spontaneity, the banter, the fun – it had all gone.

I tried to show Mick what to do but I only made things worse, then it seemed as if I was the one who was creating the problems. One day when he came home and patted Sarah on the head by way of a greeting, I said: 'Mick say something about her dress or her shoes.'

He sighed. 'Sarah,' he called. When she didn't turn he crossed the room and putting his hand under her chin, he lifted her face towards his. 'That's a pretty dress Sarah.'

'Mick, Miss Ayling said it would be better if we didn't touch Sarah like that because it gets her into bad habits. She said call her as if she was a hearing child.'

'Okay. Okay.'

'You'll have to get down to her level and speak clearly. Sarah's got to get used to reading your lips. She doesn't know what "pretty" means yet so try pointing to her dress to give her a clue.'

I desperately wanted to talk to Miss Ayling about Mick but it seemed disloyal when he wasn't there. The undercurrents and suffocating tensions which combined to make our weekends hell dissolved for me, for a while at least, when Monday came.

'Sarah's learned four new words this week Miss Ayling,' I said.

'That's very good,' she replied.

I saw then that it was, and my spirits lifted.

6.   *A warning light flashed*

'Joanne you mustn't do that,' I insisted. It was the sixth time in an hour I had tried to stop her from developing her artistic talents on the wallpaper.

Joanne waved her hand dismissively at me, blinked, and turned from me slowly in the way Sarah did when she wanted to say she couldn't see my face – and therefore couldn't lipread my words.

This one action gave Sarah power – and rendered me powerless.

It was frightening to see the way Joanne was substituting her 'normal' behaviour for Sarah's 'abnormal' kind. Because of Sarah's influence upon Joanne I asked Miss Ayling if Sarah could go to nursery school and she agreed to her going for two mornings a week. So, after visiting local nursery schools and playgroups, none of which were suitable, I went to see a small infant school eleven miles away. The headmistress, a nun from the order of the Sisters of Mercy, had first learned of Sarah's deafness through Mick's mother who used to teach in the school and, as a result, had offered Sarah a place.

It was a dour-looking building yet the classroom we entered was bright and cheerful. The walls were covered with children's paintings and there was an enormous frieze of Jack and the Beanstalk running round the room. In one corner there was a sandpit and a climbing frame; in another plasticine and paint. There was a book corner and a dressing-up corner. There were jigsaws, bricks, trains, dolls. . . . The atmosphere was happy and carefree but in an ordered way, and full of children's laughter. This was the place I had been looking for. Here they would care.

Sister kindly let me stay in the nursery every day for a week to help Sarah become accustomed to it. She wanted to help in any way she could. Joanne came with us and I couldn't have imagined a child happier than she. Nursery school was like Christmas every day. She didn't play with the children as such, but stood beside them, her face glowing with contentment.

Sarah, on the other hand, was quiet and withdrawn, rarely venturing from my side. Occasionally, I managed to persuade her to part with her 'bit of stuff' (a silky scarf) and then, providing I was in her sight, she would retire to the dressing-up corner, where, clothed in a white bridal gown, she divided her time between preening herself in the mirror and making tea for a small boy called John.

I loved watching the children in their make-believe games but Sarah stood to one side gazing at their faces, unable to join them in all but the physical sense of the word. I listened to the way the children practised their language, heard them experiment with grammar and pick up new vocabulary as though it was the easiest thing to do. One of my favourite games was a jigsaw puzzle. When the pieces were lifted they revealed the insides of a whole range of shops. I could draw endless amounts of language from this but Sarah viewed it as a pointless exercise as she did dolls and posting boxes, bricks and most of the toys. Other children who played with the jigsaw puzzle said: 'This is the butcher's shop. Now what shall I have for dinner? I'll have some chicken and some sausages.' In one game they practised hand/eye coordination, used their imagination, expanded their ideas and articulated them, and made sense of the world in which they lived.

Sarah, without someone to help her, learned hand/eye co-ordination.

Although Sarah wouldn't gain language here, she would gain a code of behaviour. She was already queuing for her milk instead of snatching it when she was thirsty. She put the toys away instead of leaving them on the floor. She raised her hand when she wanted to go to the toilet instead of holding herself and shouting loudly. She ate her food without pulling faces and she sat through the story even though she was bored.

Nursery was a welcome relief for me too, an escape from the tensions Sarah's presence brought. Even so there wasn't a moment when she was out of my thoughts, when I wasn't worrying about her, or thinking what I should be doing for her. Part of the reason for this was the nature of the work and the necessity of always being one step ahead, and part of the reason was guilt. Ever since I had read about the importance of a child's first years, I knew I had been given the last chance of helping Sarah, or to be more specific, the last chance of it having the most effect. So I shut out everything to concentrate upon her (and Joanne) because I knew I could help her. Sarah's hearing-aid had long since been transformed into a symbol of my utmost pride, not with the first word spoken but the first word she understood.

Sister asked me what it was that I wanted her and the staff to do.

'Sarah needs you to tell her each child's name over and over again. She needs you to explain what a climbing frame is for and to tell her what she is painting.' I said.

Sister had one of those faces which never looked very old but then never looked very young either.

'Sarah might understand you when you say, "Do you want some milk?" but not if you say "*Would* you like some milk?" '

The expression on Sister's face remained unchanged. I suspected that she, like Mick, thought I was creating difficulties.Even so, she made no comment, she just supported me by supporting Sarah.

I was happy to leave Sarah in this lovely school though Sarah had other ideas. I left her for only an hour at the end of the week and her screams pursued me into the playground. When I returned she was sitting in the same position as when I had left, on the nursery assistant's knee, she was sobbing, and her 'bit of stuff' was soaked from her tears.

She hadn't known I would be coming back even though I had said, 'I'll be back soon.' To her an hour was the same as for ever.

Why hadn't I listened to what Sarah was telling me?

The nursery was near the comprehensive school where Mick taught and he arranged to take Sarah to school in a friend's car so that I could use our car to pick her up at lunch-time. When our car finally broke down and Mick could no longer take her, Sarah went by taxi provided by the education authority.

I smiled encouragingly to her while she beat her fists against the taxi window and tugged frantically at the door. As it moved off her eyes were wide with fright, and her screams paralysed with panic.

I was so distraught I didn't know what to do with myself. 'She's three,' I kept saying. 'She's three. She has to go to school.'

I went into the house to relish the sound of the rare silence. I pottered for a while, moving things, chairs, cushions, ornaments, It helped a little.

Joanne followed, clutching the hem of my skirt and sucking her thumb. I bent over her and picked her up to stand her on the windowsill.

'Soon you'll be chattering and chattering,' I said, as she screwed up her nose. 'I do wish you'd hurry.'

To think I wouldn't have to teach her a word. What inconceivable bliss! I held her hands and swung her to the floor and she crawled on her knees to a scattered jigsaw-puzzle. Joanne loved all the things which Sarah didn't, games requiring patience and perseverance. Sarah's intelligence was visual and practical, it almost took a physical form. Joanne's was more cerebral.

As I went into the kitchen to wash the breakfast dishes the telephone rang. It was my friend Maureen with bad news. She had discovered that her second child, Louise, was deaf like her brother. Alan had been almost four and a half before he received his first hearing-aid although Maureen had been voicing her concern about his hearing for over *three years*.

Fear stabbed me as I replaced the receiver. I went back into the kitchen where Joanne was squeezing pastry between her fingers, and, while her back was turned, I struck a saucepan against the work surface. When Joanne spun round and smiled, the fear left me.

I had no time to dwell on Maureen's sad situation before there was a knock on the door, and, on opening it, a lady introduced herself as a health visitor.

'I've just popped in to see if you're managing,' she said. 'Is this Sarah?' She was a tall woman with dark hair and she was wearing a blue uniform.

'No, this is Joanne. Sarah's at nursery school this morning. Do come in.'

We went into the lounge and the health visitor said, 'How's Sarah doing?'

'She's fine,' I replied, stroking Joanne's hair, the feel of it soothing me. 'She knows that people talk now and she says quite a few words.' A contentment edged with exhilaration ran through me. 'Actually now you're here, would you mind having a look at Joanne for me. I just can't be certain she hears everything as she should. She had her hearing tested recently though by a teacher of the deaf. She seemed to think I was worrying unnecessarily.'

'I could arrange a test at the baby clinic,' she offered.

The appointment came within a matter of days and this time I was determined to watch everything with a critical eye. At the clinic I was asked to sit at a table with Joanne on my knee and an assistant sat opposite with a ball in her hand.

A health visitor, not the same one as before, waited for the assistant to remove the ball from the table, then she rustled some paper behind Joanne's head.

Joanne swivelled round on my knee to look at her.

Five minutes later she had responded to every sound, except one. She showed a positive lack of response to the high-frequency rattle.

And a warning light flashed in my head.

'We'll do it again,' the health visitor said, when I told her Sarah had high-frequency deafness. She was going out of her way to convince me nothing was wrong.

She shook the rattle. Joanne turned.

'We can always test Joanne another time,' the health visitor suggested, 'but I'm quite happy about her responses. Now, if we can move on. Joanne would you sit here?' She indicated a chair by the table where some toys had been arranged and Joanne slid down from my knee and went to sit on it. The health visitor put a doll in her hand and moved behind her.

Usually Joanne would swing her legs backwards and forwards but now, it seemed, she needed them for listening.

'Put the doll on the chair.'

Joanne moved her hand over the toys as if deciding where the doll should go, then she sat the doll on the chair.

Two more instructions – and Joanne began to make mistakes. In the next instruction she went completely wrong.

'I think she's had enough for one day.' The health visitor lifted Joanne down from the chair. 'You've been a good girl,' she told her. 'Your Mummy must be very proud of you.'

I wasn't listening to what she was saying. How could Joanne have followed those instructions when *I* had never asked her to do those things before?

'Now let me see.' The health visitor consulted a chart. 'What should Joanne be doing at twenty-one months? She can hold a cup, eat from a spoon, walk up steps . . .?'

'Yes.'

'. . . imitates sounds, says Mummy or Daddy, knows household items like fire, chair, kettle . . .'

It was as if time was suspended. And as the voice carried on in the background, I was thinking: but Joanne doesn't know those words. I haven't taught her them. Why haven't I taught her them?

'I'm sure there's no cause for concern,' the health visitor said, as we left the clinic.

The same evening the health visitor who had originally come to the house telephoned.

'Joanne passed the test,' I told her. 'I don't know what you think though, but she didn't respond to the high-frequency rattle the first time it was sounded, and it's left a doubt in my mind.'

'Stop worrying,' she replied. 'I'll come and test Joanne myself.'

She came a few weeks later as Mick and I were preparing to go to the zoo, and brought with her a student who was specializing in hearing impairment.

We sat Joanne at the dining-room table and she waited patiently for the test to begin. Her broderie anglaise dress was a brilliant white against her chubby suntanned arms, and her shoulder-length hair was a mass of shiny waves and intricate curls. I drew in my breath. She was beautiful.

This time the testing followed a different course. Joanne didn't respond at first and when she did it was with hesitance. She had never been this unresponsive before. It must be the tonsillitis. She got it regularly, though never as badly as Sarah, and she was always less alert during that time.

Mick watched and, as the testing progressed, he grew increasingly perturbed and kept looking to me for reassurance, a reassurance I couldn't give.

He had become extremely close to Joanne in recent months. He bathed her at night, read her a story, and played with her while I concentrated on Sarah. When I had first mentioned my concern over Joanne's hearing he had vehemently replied: 'There's nothing wrong. Her hearing's perfectly all right.' He had even helped me to test her, which had further convinced him of my hysterical need for complication in my life.

'Does Joanne talk? What does she say?' The student's voice made me turn.

'She says the odd word. I always put her on my knee when I talk to Sarah or hold her hand. I thought she would pick it up that way. . . . She has lots of friends too. I invite the children in purposely to stimulate her because of Sarah. I wish I'd talked to her on my own.' Joanne was behind in her speech because of me. She had suffered because I had concentrated on Sarah.

'Don't you worry now,' the health visitor patted my shoulder. 'I'm going to ring Mr Chapman for a full assessment. I don't care if I'm found to be wrong.'

We went to the zoo. It was the most perfect day for an outing and the sun blazed down on us. Even so Mick and I were unable to shake off the despondency we felt. The distant chords of fairground music seemed to accompany the emotions churning inside. Neither of us spoke about the test. We couldn't put our feelings into words. Perhaps it was better that way.

While Mick showed Sarah around, I pushed Joanne in her pushchair towards a bench. I had a powerful urge to be alone with her, as though this would bring comfort or solace somehow.

We must have been a hundred metres away from the elephant enclosure when an elephant trumpeted ... and Joanne turned round in her pushchair to see what had made the noise. Joyfully, I lifted her into my arms. She had heard the elephant.

Joanne had heard the elephant call.

7. *The room*

Joanne didn't know we were going to the hospital, she was just happy to be with me. I watched her through the rear-view mirror and, as she caught my eye, I winked. She laughed, screwed up her nose and blinked.

I parked the car and followed the arrows to the Hearing-Aid Department where two rows of pensioners were queuing for their right to hear. As we passed, a technician was shouting to an old man: 'You've got to turn it on. Don't forget to turn your hearing-aid on.'

In the waiting-room Joanne climbed on to my knee and began playing with the contents of my handbag. It was good to be alone with her – and yet the moments were tinged with a strange foreboding.

Panic threatened to take hold of me. Already this morning I had lost my temper with my mother who was staying with us, but even then I used the argument for giving language. 'We're *angry* Sarah,' I said. 'These are *tears*.' I lifted her finger and she touched my face. 'I'm not happy. I'm *unhappy*.' I couldn't miss such an opportunity. Sarah had to know what feelings were. I had to grasp every chance there was.

Mick and Mum had stared at me in utter disbelief as I turned from them and went into the lounge.

Joanne pulled a photograph from my bag and waved it in my face. 'That's you and Sarah,' I said. 'My babies.'

Joanne plucked at the front of her dress. 'Baabaabaa,' she chanted.

'Yes, you're wearing the same dress now. It's blue,' I pointed to the material, 'and red'.

I kissed her soft cheek and, leaning against me, she wriggled her bottom further into my lap. As I held her the anxieties of the past months weighed heavily on my shoulders. Today they would all be dispelled.

Lifting her hand, Joanne began circling the palm with my finger. I used to do that with Sarah. 'Round and round the garden like a teddy bear.' It had puzzled, then annoyed me when she wouldn't join in the rhyme.

Joanne's thumb and forefinger moved up my arm, the thumb still wet from sucking. I pointed to the photo. 'There's a kitten,' I said. 'Isn't he sweet?'

Joanne hunched her shoulders and, clicking her tongue, she stroked the top of her mouth to tell me the kitten had whiskers.

In the photo Joanne was smiling, always ready to please; Sarah looked shyer, more self-conscious. It showed Joanne as one who took life as it came and welcomed every minute; Sarah a child who approached it with hesitance, almost with suspicion. Was that what life had taught them? Joanne to trust, Sarah to distrust? For how many times in the past had I scolded Sarah for doing something she didn't know was wrong? How often had she pushed me to the limits of my endurance until my patience snapped? It had happened only yesterday when she had refused to have her hair brushed. It was always a struggle. A fight to clean her teeth, wash her hair, tie her shoe-laces, wipe her hands, or blow her nose. This time I had simply had enough. I held her down and pulled the brush through her hair. When I let her go, Sarah deliberately messed it up again.

'I'm warning you Sarah. You're going to have your hair brushed.' She had started screaming in her usual hysterical fashion and run for the door. I caught her and brushed her hair. She messed it. I brushed it. She messed it.

Of course I should have stopped there, pretended it wasn't important, but Sarah's open defiance, the look on her face, her dismissive hand movements and screeching voice, made me boil inside. After that every spit, kick, scream and howl was like a screw turning in my brain until I lost control. I got hold of Sarah's shoulders and shook her and shook her and shook her, and if I hadn't done that I would have smacked her and smacked her and smacked her.

And when I had finished shaking her, Sarah reached up . . . and messed her hair.

In the months since the photo was taken Joanne's hair had grown thick and long, and she wore it in many different styles. Whenever I tried to grow Sarah's the ends went fuzzy because it was so fine. I looked at my watch. Why didn't they hurry up?

As if in answer to my request the swing doors were flung open and a voice said 'Joanne?'

I looked up to see the same grey-haired nurse as before smiling at us. She held her hand out to Joanne, and Joanne slid down from my knee.

Waves of panic surged through me again keeping me pinned to the chair. I rummaged through my handbag as though there was something important there. I found a handkerchief and blew my nose. I studied the appointment card. I put the photograph away. Finally I raised my head and smiled at the nurse standing hand in hand with Joanne, both of them waiting for me.

The nurse led us down the corridor, past curtained cubicles. The room, the one in which Mr Chapman waited, was getting nearer, yet the corridor seemed long. My throat tightened and my steps faltered. The urge to turn was so strong that I had to use all my strength to fight it. When we stopped walking the nurse leaned forward, and opened the last pair of doors.

And there it was. The scene which had tormented me for so long: the silent figures, the table, the chair, the pegboard wall. Even the light dazzled in the way it had nine months before. The grey carpet tiles seemed to come forward to meet me, urging me on. It was one step too many, now it could never be retrieved.

Mr Chapman moved forward to introduce me to the consultant dressed in a white coat. 'Why have you brought Joanne?' the consultant asked sharply.

His question took me aback. 'I think Joanne may have a hearing loss,' I said, struggling for an answer. 'Not severe like Sarah's,' I added quickly. 'Maybe a partial hearing loss.'

I sat down, all strength drained from me. I had never expressed such a thought before but in justifying my reason for being here, my words had an awful ring of truth about them.

There were a few people sitting opposite my chair; Miss Ayling (my teacher), the female doctor as before, the jolly nurse, and the assistant who helped Mr Chapman do the testing. I smiled at them, and they smiled back at me, but I could tell by their expressions they were thinking of other children they could be seeing, ones like Sarah, not ones who could hear.

Joanne seemed tiny on my knee as she sat with her back straight, strictly to attention. Sarah was alert, Joanne more so, but in a different kind of way. Her curls were clustered at the nape of her neck where they had escaped from their hair slides. I noticed a sock had slipped down, and, as I pulled it up, I couldn't resist touching her suntanned leg.

Mr Chapman moved behind our chair and his assistant rose from her seat to crouch on the carpet in front of us.

The rattle sounded. After a moment Joanne turned towards it and, when Mr Chapman patted her on the shoulder to tell her she had done well, she positively glowed.

He rustled some paper next. Joanne moved as though to turn, then hesitated before turning to me as if she needed confirmation of the sound.

'We'll do that again,' Mr Chapman told the assistant.

Joanne stiffened in readiness. She was trying, really concentrating on listening.

I ached for her to turn, and finally she did. 'You're a good girl,' the assistant said.

Joanne smiled shyly as if she found praise embarrassing, when really I was sure she loved being the centre of attention.

'I think we'll do some more tests,' Mr Chapman told me after a while. He went to the cupboard and after selecting a boat, he showed Joanne to the small chair Sarah had once sat on. Joanne smiled happily when she recognized the toy because she had played the game many times with me at home. She picked up one of the little wooden men and waited for the command, her hand poised in mid-air.

Mr Chapman laughed. 'She's played this game before,' he said. Then his face grew serious again.

'Go,' he said loudly.

Joanne placed the man in the boat and picked up the next one.

'Go.'

Joanne confidantly put the man in the front of the boat, then changing her mind, she moved him to the back. Satisfied with his position she touched each little man on the head with her finger as though she was counting them. She picked up the next one.

'go.'

And that was when the atmosphere in the room changed. There was a deathly hush as we waited for Joanne. I wanted, as I had never wanted anything in my life before, I wanted her to put the man in the boat. Her hand was chubby and babyish as it clasped the wooden figure . . . and waited for the command.

'Go.'

Joanne put the man in the boat.

I stopped myself from moaning aloud but it still went on in my head as I felt myself slipping down down down. I had seen Miss Ayling's face as it recognized the truth. I looked from one face to another and saw them all trying to disguise their shock. Dear God they knew too.

The testing carried on far away from me as if I wasn't part of it. No sound penetrated, no sight registered, no thought stirred.

I became aware of Mr Chapman lifting a chair and crossing the room. My head began screaming as if to create a barrier between him and me. I wanted to force him back with my screams as though they were palpable electrifying things. Anything not to hear his words.

Some distant part of me felt sorry for him. It couldn't be easy to have to say:

'Mrs Robinson. Joanne's hearing is impaired.'

This time it was too much to take.

Afterwards, I turned from Mr Chapman to look at Joanne, to see for myself that it was true. Her shoulders couldn't carry this burden. Deafness was too big. It would hurt her. Oh why couldn't it be me? I could cope. *Please* not Joanne. Not Joanne.

She was kneeling on my lap, facing me, and her head was on one side as she watched the tears rolling down my cheeks. I saw Miss Ayling coming towards me. She placed a white handkerchief on my shoulder and, when I didn't move, Joanne picked it up and gently, very gently, she wiped the tears from my face and stroked my cheek with her hand. It was as though she was saying: 'Don't cry for me Mummy.'

That moment was the lowest point in my life.

What was to become of us?

We arrived home to find my mother hanging nappies on the line.

'I thought you'd be back ages ago,' she said.

I started walking towards the door, then stopped. 'Joanne's deaf,' I said without looking at her.

I couldn't let her come near me. I could only keep going if I put some barrier up against my feelings. Allow nothing to penetrate.

Mum followed me indoors. 'Kathy. How could she be? Who says she is? It's not possible.'

Mum went to her bedroom and the sound of music blaring led me to the lounge where Sarah was watching a cartoon on the television. I turned the volume down, lifted Joanne on to the settee beside her, and went into the kitchen to wait for Mick. The minutes dragged by, yet, when I heard the door handle, it made me jump.

Mick's eyes went *straight* to mine – and immediately he knew. But it still had to be said.

I didn't wait for him to take his jacket off, didn't make him a cup of tea, I just stood there and said it.

'Joanne's deaf.'

Mick put his hand to his forehead and his face drained of colour. His eyes filled. 'Not Joanne,' he said. 'Not Joanne.'

For some reason I remembered something Mr Chapman once told me. 'When I tell parents their child is hearing-impaired,' he had said, 'I can feel their hatred. I'm the one who has given their child deafness.'

I had never felt that way though I wondered vaguely if perhaps Mick now hated me.

He raised his head, averting his eyes. 'Where's Jo?'

'Watching television.'

'I want to see her,' he said, and went out of the kitchen.

Tea-time came and we went through the motions. No one talked about Joanne. We said polite things like 'Pass me the jam please,' and 'Would you like tea or coffee?' Here, at a time when we should have been able to comfort each other, we could not. It would have only taken one move on my part, but it seemed as if I was cut off from them. There was a whole afternoon between us, and I suppose many months before that as well.

Mick needed me but what could I offer? I felt nothing. When I had told him about Joanne, I put my hand on his shoulder, but it was a gesture only and held no comfort.

In the same situation Mum would have been kind and loving. She wouldn't have done what I was doing to her. Yet she was the very source of the persistence and force of character which I was having to develop in my dealings with Sarah.

Later, Mick took Sarah and Joanne to bed and he was upstairs a very long time. When he came down again he had changed into jeans and a grey jumper.

'I'm just going out for a while,' he said.

'Where to?'

'I don't know. I have to get out of this house.'

When he had gone I went into the lounge where Mum was sitting and said, 'Would you mind if I went to bed?'

'Do you want to talk Kathy?'

'I don't think I can. I'd rather be on my own.'

I lay in bed for a long while looking up at the ceiling. In time the barren feeling began to lift and sadness descended like a cloud in the dark. Then I wept. Not for myself as I had with Sarah. I wept for Joanne.

8. *A resolve*

On Monday Mick went to work and four walls closed in around me.

'Gamma gong in car,' Sarah said.

'Yes, Grandma went home to see Grandpa.'

Sarah folded her arms across her chest, then glancing at me, she checked they were in the right position. Giggling, she poked Joanne and when she had her attention, folded her arms over a large, quite imaginary bosom.

Joanne tutted as if reprimanding her and having established her loyalty to me, she held out her hand in a bold demand for sweets.

I laughed at the glint in her eyes, but the feeling of helplessness was still overwhelming. I didn't know where to begin. I didn't know how to begin.

When Miss Ayling came she gave me one of her penetrating looks and said, 'Kathy, I'm sorry.'

She didn't say any more. She was one of those rare people who really understood, and when that happens words aren't necessary.

I cried a little, then dried my tears. Emotion mustn't be allowed to interfere with what had to be done.

'What are we going to do?' I was in Miss Ayling's hands and, if she didn't know, it was the end for us.

'I've been thinking,' she said, as she straightened the pleats of her skirt. 'We'll try them side by side and see how it works. I've brought an auditory training unit with me,' and she put it on the table next to the other one.

We sat Joanne on a cushion next to Sarah on one side of the table with the earphones on, Joanne's swamping her, and we sat opposite with a microphone each.

The lesson was short and simple, just right for Joanne, Sarah had heard it all before. Miss Ayling was pleased it had gone so well, but I held reservations. Sarah had a reasonably wide understanding of language by now and she was saying quite a few words. I just couldn't bring myself to start at the beginning again.

The lesson went over and over in my mind long after Miss Ayling had left. Joanne needed to know the names of things and how they worked, whereas Sarah was on to the 'whys' and 'wherefores'. How could I give them both what they needed in the same breath?

In the end I decided that I would aim the lesson at Sarah's level of understanding but explain everything in such a way that the *meaning* was clear to Joanne, even if the words were too difficult for her.

Over the next week I worked hard to find a balance but was forced to admit defeat. My problem was not one of language, but of two small children, one of whom hadn't the slightest intention of letting the other learn. The possibilities Sarah now had for undermining me were an endless source of amusement to her.

'Here's a glass,' I said.

Sarah yawned.

Joanne looked towards her, and *away* from me.

'I'll pour some water *into* the glass.'

Sarah picked up a pencil and 'smoked' it.

Joanne giggled.

'Now I'll pour some water *out* of the glass.'

Sarah raised her little finger.

Joanne copied her.

'I'll put the glass on my *head*.'

Joanne clapped her hands and begged for more.

Sarah drummed her fingers on the table and looked at me discerningly. 'I'm not taken in by you,' her expression seemed to say. 'It's *still* work – and it's *still* boring.'

I had been given a fawn-coloured hearing-aid for Joanne. It was small and curved to fit behind her ear.

'I'm relieved it's not like Sarah's,' Mick said when he first saw it. 'I don't think I could have faced taking them both out with hearing-aids on their chests.'

I was as relieved as he, not so much for the look of the aid, as the size. A small aid meant Joanne didn't need the power of a body-worn aid.

The ear mould arrived through the post and I brought Joanne's ear-level aid out of the cupboard and showed it to her for the first time. Her reaction was revealing. I hadn't realized, until I saw her overjoyed face, that she had viewed Sarah's appendage as her loss. By not having a hearing-aid *she* had been the one who was different.

A moment later Sarah and Joanne had put their heads together and were examining the aid in detail. They switched it on and off, turned up the volume till it whistled, found where the battery was kept and pondered over its size. When the inspection was complete, Sarah indicated, by a tiny jerk of the head, that she wanted to put the ear mould in Joanne's ear, and Joanne obediently allowed her ear to be manhandled by Sarah.

'I'll do it, you watch,' I said, pointing to my eyes.

Joanne held her head on one side for me and I fitted the ear mould, turning it until it was snugly into position, then sandwiched the aid behind her ear. Joanne turned round to show Sarah – and the aid flopped forward over her ear.

Sarah raised an eyebrow. Hearing-aids were swapped. And while the body-aid hung loosely on Joanne's chest, Sarah strutted round the kitchen vehemently insisting that she could hear. Her face glowed with the certainty of better hearing and, considering it was no use to her whatever, I was impressed by the ease with which she could lie.

Over the next two days the aid's novelty began to pall and interest reverted to the bathroom once more. So when I heard hysterical laughter coming from that direction, I ran upstairs as fast as I could.

I pushed open the door to see two children standing side by side peering into the lavatory – the sound of flushing water dying away.

'What have you done?' I demanded of Sarah with outstretched palms and query written into my expression.

Sarah pointed to Joanne and gaily mimed her taking off her hearing-aid, putting it down the lavatory pan, and pulling the handle.

My heart plummeted. 'Joanne you tell me.'

With great relish Joanne began to give me her side of the story. I gathered that Sarah had wanted to know if Joanne's ear-level aid would sink or float and Joanne had, at Sarah's instigation, dropped the aid into the lavatory. It sank. Then, Sarah told Joanne to pull the handle and oh – this was shown by two hands clutched to her mouth and an intake of breath – the hearing-aid 'Ga gone'.

All was explained in a parade of hand movements, while her face moved through a range of emotions covering curiosity, agreement, query, delight, surprise and astonishment. And nowhere did I see a trace of guilt, nor one flicker of repentance.

I turned to Sarah but her face was as innocent as her conscience was clear. She nodded, giving me the go-ahead to tell Joanne off.

What on earth was I going to tell the technician at the hospital? What was Sarah up to telling Joanne to put her aid down the lavatory? As I thought about it, suspicion began to cross my mind. Joanne had been getting a lot of attention lately: as much as Sarah in fact. Why, the clever little madam. Not only had Sarah managed to dispose of the offending aid in quite an ingenious way, she had also fixed it so that Joanne would get the blame.

It was with some trepidation I faced the hospital technician that afternoon. I couldn't tell him the truth, for he was a forbidding little man, and so I told him I had mislaid the aid.

He looked at his records and muttered something about 'Mothers who let their children roam the streets for hours losing their hearing-aids and putting their ear moulds down drains'.

Asking for a new lead or battery was always an ordeal. Ear moulds never fitted properly, batteries quickly expired, and leads broke easily. We were only ever allowed one spare battery and Sarah even managed to dispose of that with a certain inventiveness. . . .

As we arrived home Joanne's hearing-aid battery ran out. I took the precious spare from my handbag and put it on the side while I removed the old battery from Joanne's aid. Then I heard Sarah scream. I turned to see her transfixed to the spot, her eyes pleading with me. Frantically, she pointed to her nose and when I looked, there, about to disappear, was one brand-new national health battery.

'Breathe *down* your nose,' I said, pointing downwards. 'Joanne, move out of the way.' Joanne was peering up Sarah's nostril and this was neither the time nor the place.

Sarah tried to do as I asked her but her control was slipping.

By now the battery was almost out of sight and, as I didn't dare risk trying to dislodge it, I put Sarah in the car, with Joanne, and headed for the local hospital. On the way Sarah sneezed, and the battery landed on her lap.

No more mishaps occurred in the next two hours and after tea I prepared for the final lesson. There were two lollipops to put on the table, two auditory training units, two sets of earphones. There were two microphones to hang round my neck, and four controls which needed to be adjusted to four different hearing losses in four different ears. When everything was ready and Joanne and Sarah were sitting down, Joanne's hand strayed to the tempting array of knobs before her.

Sarah smacked it. 'Goaa gauky curl.'

'Joanne's not a naughty girl Sarah,' I said, seeing the lesson getting out of hand before it had even started. 'Here, let me try your earphones.'

Sarah passed them to me and I put them on my head to check they were working properly. I had just turned the volume on when Sarah leaned over the table and shrieked into the microphone round my neck. Her shriek was magnified many many times over and while I was holding my head and rocking, Sarah and Joanne scrambled down from the table.

End of lesson.

'Perhaps you could try them separately,' suggested Miss Ayling.

I put Joanne to bed and worked with Sarah and while I worked with Joanne, I put Sarah in a playpen with her toys. Sarah screamed blue murder at her imprisonment, making it impossible to concentrate, so in the end I lifted her out on the strict understanding she did *not* interrupt. Sarah stood by my side sucking her finger as I worked with Joanne, and believe it or not, she kept her promise.

It was natural my whole instinct should lean towards Sarah simply because she needed me the most. As I was aware of this inclination, I made a resolve to give the same amount of time to Joanne as I gave to Sarah – and to be seen to do so. It was only right; besides, something told me if I didn't do it there would be repercussions later. So if I gave ten minutes to Sarah, I gave ten minutes to Joanne. If I spoke to Sarah, I repeated my words to Joanne. The work was then doubled. I had to do in one day for two children what had previously taken a whole day for one.

Any remaining vestige of confidence in myself as a mother had been swept away with Joanne's diagnosis. I was beset with self-doubt. Is this the right way to do it? What shall I do next? Is there something more I could have done, more I could have said? Even simple decisions about food and clothing were impossible to make and only loomed as further evidence of my shameful inability to cope.

If Miss Ayling was important before, now her visits were the only light in a dark week. I accepted that she knew what she was doing without question, that she knew more than Mick or I what was necessary for our children. Each faltering step I took was initiated by Miss Ayling and it was only she who gave me the strength to continue.

If Miss Ayling gave me strength, it was Mr Chapman who gave me hope when I felt there was none. 'Whatever you put in,' he said, 'you'll get back. Maybe not for a long time. But you will get it back.'

'Are you sure? Everything?' I questioned.

'Yes.'

It was as simple as that.

9.   *Mandy*

I opened my arms to Sarah as she climbed into our bed and for once her warm, acquiescent body cuddled close to mine.

'She'll have to stay in her own room,' Mick said the following morning. 'It'll get to be a habit.' And a habit with Sarah was impossible to break. For months we tried to persuade her to stay in her own room; the light was left on for her, we changed her nappy when we went to bed. (She still wore one at night.) She had a drink by her side, toys next to her pillow. Nothing worked. Sometimes she came into us once, more often twice, occasionally five times. Every attempt to remove her was followed by a prolonged, harrowing tantrum.

When she joined us again at some unmentionable hour, I let her go to sleep before attempting to move her. When her breathing deepened, I slid my hand under her and began to lift. Immediately Sarah sat up, and screamed.

Woken from the depths of sleep, Mick also sat up with a dazed expression on his face.

I lifted Sarah over my shoulder and while she screamed and stretched her arms out towards the bed, I carried her back to her own room. I put her on the bed, pulled my nightie from her grasp, and ran to shut the door before she could escape. She ran after me, tugging at the handle, screaming, sobbing, and catching her breath.

Her screams were unlike anything I had heard before. 'Sarah. Shhh. Daddy's asleep.'

Why was she like this? Other three-year-olds had to sleep in their own beds. If I gave in now Sarah would scream twice as long tomorrow night when I put her back. If I gave in now it would be the beginning of the end. She would want her own way with everything. If only we could come to a compromise but there was no middle way with Sarah. It was all or nothing.

In Sarah's bedroom I reached up to the shelf above her bed for one of her dolls. 'Sarah.' I shook my hand in the air to attract her attention and when she turned her tear-stained face towards me, I rocked the doll in my arms.

Sarah eyed me as if I was insane. Dolls were objects to her like ornaments were to me. And no one in their right mind cradles ornaments.

I went to lift her, but she became like a dead weight. A change of tactics was needed. I lay down on her bed and after considering this move, she decided to join me. I stroked her forehead as she sucked her 'bit of stuff'. She shrugged my hand away. I rested it on her shoulder very lightly. She chose to ignore it. Ages afterwards, her eyes began to close and as her white and wrinkled finger slid slowly from her mouth, I removed my hand from her shoulder. Sarah's eyes opened.

She wailed as I left the room, then she screamed in fury. Mick groaned when my feet touched his and burying his head in the pillow he muttered, 'I've got to get up in the morning.'

The screaming stopped, and there was silence. I heard a bed creak. Footsteps sounded on the carpet. Before Sarah could cross the room I had swept her into my arms, and an ear-splitting scream rent the air.

Mick sat up in bed again. 'I have children all day,' he said, his voice thick with sleep, and, pulling back the bedclothes he stood up, 'now we have this every night as well. There's never any peace in this house.' He picked up his pillow and went to the door. 'I'm going in the spare room.'

'You think it's me that's causing all the problems don't you?' I shouted after him. What was the matter with me? Other mothers didn't have children who behaved like this.

The birds were singing by the time I managed to settle Sarah in her own bed, but, in the morning light, I woke to find her asleep beside me.

Mick came into the bedroom and kissed me. 'I'm sorry,' he said as he pulled on his shirt. 'Let's start again.' He looked down at Sarah who was curled up in the sheets, an angelic expression on her face. 'Poor old Sarah.'

'I hated you last night.'

'I know you did.'

Getting out of bed, I went into Joanne's room to find her leaning over the side of the cot swishing the curtains.

'Joanne,' I called from the middle of the room.

'JOANNE . . . . JOANNE.'

I shouted her name as loudly as I could until I was yelling it, and still she made no move to look in my direction. Her cot was filled with the toys and books she had pulled from the shelf and her pink musical-box was playing 'Here we go round the mulberry bush'. She must have seen my reflection in the window because she turned round and shrieked with happiness at seeing me. I hugged her and put her hearing-aid on.

'Hello Joanne. *Good morning.*'

Joanne was learning language in the way I imagine a hearing child might. She absorbed it. She understood it. She remembered it. She spoke it. Language was a living joy to her. Why it should be this way with Joanne and not with Sarah is, I believe, to do with the early years. Hearing something in the first two years of Joanne's life had been better than hearing nothing at all, which is what happened to Sarah. Some stimulation had been better than no stimulation. It could be that this had helped to keep the nerve pathways in Joanne's brain open, alert, ready. And it could have been that even a little sound was enough to provide the foundations for learning language. Joanne would have heard intonation in our voices, providing we were close to her and speaking loudly, and intonation is a communication, an exchange. Now when Joanne wore her auditory training unit, there was a direct link as I spoke, no barriers to stop the flow of my voice from reaching her.

Deafness was different for Sarah. Sarah had difficulty in re-membering words. This is why I always gave her a 'peg' for each word, something in her experience to help her recall it by. If I introduced the word 'cottage' for instance, I would say: 'Grandma and Grandpa have a cottage.' Then I would show her a photo and compare it to other forms of houses.

Apart from her memory there was the matter of the profound degree of her deafness. Perhaps it was this which made the difference to the way language was acquired. If so perhaps I was expecting too much of Sarah. I asked her to hear what was impossible for her to hear, lipread sounds which couldn't be seen on the lips, and then, together with the expressions on my face, the way I gestured and what little she could hear and lipread, I asked that she assemble this information in her brain like a mixed-up jigsaw puzzle with pieces missing, and then make sense of it all. Finally, I asked that this same information be repeated, not in the way she heard, saw, or felt it, but in words.

Whole words.

Joanne had climbed out of her cot and was standing with

her face towards the wall hiding something. It was a blue wax crayon.

'Go and see Sarah,' I said to distract her. 'Wake her up.'

'Kerwah.' Joanne repeated Sarah's name and rising up on tiptoe, placed a finger on her mouth. As a siren would have had difficulty waking Sarah, I thought Joanne most considerate.

We found Sarah sitting up in bed stretching. I didn't bother putting her hearing-aid on before I said, '*Good morning* Sarah,' because her lipreading, of necessity, was better than Joanne's lipreading. '*Good morning*,' I repeated. Then to remind her of what this meant, I added: '*Hello.*'

I lifted Joanne on to the bed beside her and pulled the hearing-aid harness over Sarah's shoulders. Lipreading alone was such a hit-and-miss affair and I would feel easier in my mind once I knew that my voice was making contact with her. 'You've *been* asleep,' I told her and yawned. 'Not asleep *now*.' I lay on the bed and closed my eyes. 'You've *been* asleep. You and Joanne are going to *wash* your faces.' I rubbed my cheeks.

Sarah looked at Joanne and immediately they crossed their arms in outright refusal. And there was no way of reasoning or appealing to their better natures even. I hadn't realized how powerful words were until words were no longer at my disposal.

Only after I had done three gambols across the bedroom carpet would they come. In the bathroom I held a toothbrush near my mouth. '*Brush* your teeth.' I motioned a 'brushing' movement. 'This is *striped* toothpaste. Sarah this is *striped* toothpaste.'

'Dame me.' Joanne pointed to her pyjamas.

'Good girl. The *same* as you. Your pyjamas are striped too. Sarah. Your pyjamas are *striped*.' I ran my finger down the stripes. 'The toothpaste is *striped*.' I held the toothpaste against her pyjamas. 'They're the *same*.'

'Aaiee,' Sarah said, her voice ending on a high note.

'Yes, the same.' I understood every word Sarah said because I had taught her every word she was able to say.

'Joanne. Hold the *handle* of the toothbrush. Not the brush part,' I pointed and shook my head. 'The *handle*.'

I took Joanne's toothbrush from her and held it to my mouth. 'It's *bristly* like a hairbrush.' I motioned brushing my hair. '*Bristly.*' I rubbed the bristles against her hand.

'Sarah. The toothbrush is *bristly*. Feel it.' Sarah held out the palm of her hand and I rubbed the bristles on it. 'It's *bristly* like a hairbrush.' I picked up a hairbrush. '*Bristles.*'

'Daee iyee.' Sarah stroked her chin.

'Very good girl. Daddy's *chin* is *bristly* too.' It was wonderful when Sarah led me rather than the other way round. 'Joanne. Daddy's *chin* is bristly.'

Joanne felt her chin and pretended that it prickled.

Sarah turned towards the basin. I banged two shampoo bottles together and when she looked round, I hid them behind my back. 'You *listen*.' I banged the bottles again, first behind her head for her to hear the sound, and then in front of her so she could see what had made it.

'Goaa baah.'

'Shall I bang them for *Joanne*?'

'Goaa baah,' Sarah nodded.

We emerged from the bathroom half an hour later not a great deal cleaner but smelling a whole lot sweeter. Sarah and Joanne had after-shave on their chins, deodorant under their arms, and for some reason on their chests as well. They had perfume behind their ears and hair spray on every part of their bodies except their hair. They had sticking-plaster on their knees. Sarah had a patch over one eye and Joanne's arm was in a sling made from a nappy. By some miracle we were also dressed.

'Pooh what a pong,' Mick said coming upstairs, using words I would never attempt to introduce. In this way he was far more natural than me.

'That's my after-shave.' He patted his recently shaved face.

'Goaa.' Joanne jumped up and down shouting her name.

'It's *my* after-shave.'

'Kerwah.' Sarah banged her chest as she said her name too.

'It's for my face Sarah, not your face.' Mick's earlier self-consciousness about talking to Sarah was beginning to ease.

Joanne laughed. Sarah's eyes twinkled, though her face was straight.

Mick kissed us goodbye and after we had waved to him from the window, we stayed to watch the children passing on their way to school. Two girls went by with their arms linked and I wondered if I could somehow introduce the idea of friendship to Sarah. Miss Ayling had said I must not be afraid of introducing concepts yet I had been stuck on 'fun' for weeks now. 'We're having *fun* Sarah. This is *fun*. You enjoy swimming. It's *fun*.'

'Sarah,' I said, keeping within Joanne's sight. 'Those two girls like each other.' I drew my index fingers together to indicate closeness. 'They're *friends*.'

Sarah looked deeply into my eyes as if it was there she might fathom the secret of my words. She nodded, willing me to explain, then drew her index fingers together to tell me it was 'that bit' she wasn't sure about.

'They're *friends*. They play together.' I skipped. 'They work together at school.' I scribbled with my finger on the window ledge. 'They go swimming together.' I 'swam' with my hands. 'They do everything together.' I made two circles in the air. 'Sarah, they *like* each other.'

Sarah nodded to say she understood now. She went to the side window and pointed towards a small girl who was standing in her garden two doors away from us. Mandy was about four years old and she often came to play with Sarah and Joanne. She was a quiet sensitive child who never had much to say. With Sarah and Joanne she showed a tolerance and patience beyond her years. Sarah's day wasn't complete until she had seen Mandy. Mandy's friendship was the most important thing in the world to her.

Sarah drew her index fingers together and banged her chest as she said her own name. 'Kerwah.'

'Yes Sarah. Mandy is *your friend*,' I said in answer to her question.

It was as though I had given Sarah the sun, the moon and the stars. As if she had waited all her life for this word without knowing until now what it was she had been missing. Her face was alive with comprehension, and shining, positively shining.

She ran to the door and when I opened it for her, she went down the steps as fast as she could, to run along the path to where Mandy was standing. Mandy smiled and Sarah nodded an acknowledgement. They stood side by side for a moment, then Sarah, glancing shyly at Mandy, linked arms with her.

Now she had a friend too.

I lifted Joanne on to my hip and we went out to join them. There was little to disturb the peace except for someone whistling and the distant cries of seagulls. In the gardens opposite us, a celebratory crown of flowers was patterned on the slope. During the day, holidaymakers strolled through the gardens on their way to the beach and they always stopped to admire the flowers.

Mandy went indoors and I stood Sarah and Joanne on the wall outside our house. They watched me expectantly, Joanne in pink dungarees, Sarah in a pale-green, patterned dress.

'*Jump* down,' I said, and staggered as first Sarah, and then Joanne, threw themselves into my arms.

In the last few days I had discovered that if I used words and actions together, Sarah learned quickly. If she could 'feel' words, she could retain words, and when she wished to recall, there was the memory of movement to help her. Each hour that passed opened my eyes to some new aspect of learning I had not been aware of before.

'Let's go to the shops,' I suggested. 'We'll buy one, *two*, lollipops.' I held up two fingers.

Joanne held up three fingers hopefully.

Joanne lay in the pushchair on the way to the village while Sarah walked beside me taking in the sights. It was almost as if the deprivation of one sense made the others demand more stimulation as compensation, because nothing, no matter how small, escaped her attention. As we approached the centre of the village, she saw a bald man crossing the road and a look of bewilderment came over her face. She felt her head and said: 'Gog gone Goaa.'

'It's all gone Joanne,' I explained, and she reached up and felt all over her head too.

Sarah by this time was miming a man having great difficulty finding hairs on his head.

Joanne laughed and laughed, and the man abruptly changed direction.

This sort of thing was happening with increasing regularity. Anyone who strayed from what Sarah considered 'normal' – people with buck teeth, long noses, frizzy hair, no teeth – immediately became the object of her wickedly witty and invariably mocking sense of humour. When she discussed these characteristics with Joanne, their gesturing was so obvious everyone knew who they were 'gossiping' about.

At home if Sarah wanted to talk about a particular person, she wouldn't use his or her name, but an identifiable mannerism, which she then exaggerated. She would have us rolling on our chairs with laughter as she mimicked a whole range of relations and friends; their walks, the way they stood, how they jingled their money in their pocket, ran their fingers through their hair, sniffed, or even blew their noses.

We reached the shops without seeing any more bald men but, on entering the butcher's, Sarah promptly embarrassed an elderly gentlemen by pointing to his hearing-aid and shouting at the top of her voice, 'Dame, dame,' then jabbing her own ear with her finger.

'Yes, it's the *same* as yours,' I said, moving between Sarah and the man, who was trying hard to ignore her.

In the chemist's she embarrassed me by crossing her legs, holding herself, and shouting 'Pooh'. As I removed her from the shop I wondered if she would still be as indiscreet at sixteen.

Outside the sweetshop, she embarrassed me again by scowling at a friend who had stopped to talk to me, blaming her for delaying our trip into the sweetshop. For today Sarah was going to buy her own sweets for the first time ever. I had chosen this particular shop for Sarah's introduction to the big wide world because the lady in it spoke clearly. I crouched before Sarah. 'Stay here a moment. I'm coming back.'

I opened the door of the shop and hesitantly approached the lady behind the counter. 'I wonder if you would help me?' I asked. I didn't want to say the word 'deaf' but telling the lady that Sarah was 'hearing-impaired' only gave half the story.

'Sarah is deaf.'

I had said it. Saying the word would never be so difficult again.

I pointed to Sarah through the window. 'I want her to be confident in shops later on. Would you mind if she came to buy some sweets on her own?'

The lady smiled reassuringly and after I had asked her to face Sarah when she came in so that she could lipread, and told her she would be asking for two lollipops, I went back to Sarah.

'Say to the lady, "Can I have two lollipops please?" '

'Wowwi.'

'Yes. *Lollipops.*'

Clutching her money tightly in her hand, and looking exceedingly important, Sarah pushed open the door. She walked straight up to the lady and held out her hand. The lady bent over her and said something which I gather Sarah didn't understand, because the lady blushed as she repeated her words. Sarah pointed to the glass counter, and when the lady held up two lollipops, Sarah nodded. The lady put them in a bag, then went to the till and rang the money in, before coming round to the other side of the counter again to give Sarah her change. At the door Sarah gave the lady a little wave. The lady waved back.

Sarah emerged from the shop smiling proudly. She handed me the money and, after comparing the lollipops, chose one for Joanne: the smaller of course.

I wouldn't forget the lady. Not only had she helped Sarah, and would do so again, but she had made it easier for me to ask for help in the future.

10. *An impenetrable shell*

'Goaa gauky curl go gone biee.'

'Joanne is a naughty girl because the biscuits have all gone? Oh Sarah, I do love you.' I bent to hug her but she shrugged my hands away.

'Goaa gauky curl,' she repeated as she wagged her finger, a self-righteous little smile on her lips.

Manipulating the truth (and getting Joanne into trouble) was Sarah's favourite occupation. It gave her a marvellous sense of power and appealed to her sense of humour. She blamed everyone for her misdeeds from the tortoise next door to Grandma miles away. I couldn't make her see that this was wrong. She would probably grow up doing and saying whatever she felt like at the time.

Sarah was still blaming Joanne for eating the biscuits when the doorbell rang. It was my neighbour. She wanted to use the telephone as her five-year-old son Simon, who hadn't been at school very long, had just turned up at home.

Sarah started tugging at my skirt. Even at three years and eight months of age, she did not like being excluded from conversation.

'Bummy,' she said when the neighbour had gone. She raised her shoulders and spread the palms of her hands questioningly, though no hint of a question entered her voice.

I wondered, when I saw her eagerness, whether I could some-how tell her what my neighbour had said using the words Sarah understood and miming the rest. I thought for a moment . . . 'Simon.'

Sarah nodded her head in anticipation.

'Simon is a naughty boy. His Mummy loves him but he has been naughty.' I wagged my finger and smacked my leg. 'He wouldn't eat his dinner.' I mimed 'eating' then pushing my plate from me as if in disgust. I shook my head adamantly, and folded my arms.

Sarah stopped sucking her finger and her eyes, big blue dips in the ocean, stared up at me. She took a step nearer, and I felt excitement grow. Sarah had never shown such an interest in anything I had to tell her before.

'Gauky Kerwah.'

'Naughty like Sarah? No, you're not naughty.'

'Gauky aauma.'

'Was Simon naughty at *home*? No, he was naughty at school.'

Sarah drew in her breath and shook her head slowly from side to side as if to say, 'I can't believe what I'm hearing!'

I mimed Simon going to school in the morning, waving goodbye to his mother at the gate, taking off his blazer, and sitting down at his desk to write.

Sarah moved her hand, wanting me to continue.

I mimed him sitting down to dinner with the other children. I mimed them eating their dinner. 'Simon would not eat his dinner. He said "No".'

Sarah's mouth fell open. 'Kimo pea.'

'No, Simon would *not* eat his *peas*.'

I could have kissed her. 'Simon wouldn't eat his *peas*. He wouldn't eat his *meat*.' I opened the fridge and held up some meat. '*Meat*. Simon wouldn't eat his potatoes.' I went to the cupboard and showed Sarah a potato. '*Potato.*'

'Pogaco,' Sarah whispered.

'Yes, potato. Simon said, "No dinner today".' I drew myself up straight and frowned. 'Simon's teacher was very *angry*.'

Sarah smacked her leg.

'No, she didn't smack him. Simon left school and ran home to his Mummy.' I ran on the spot.

Sarah raised a finger.

'Yes, he was on his own. By *himself*.'

'Kimo gauky,' she said, her face wreathed in smiles.

Suddenly all was revealed to me.

Now Sarah wasn't the only naughty child in the world . . . because Simon was too.

When Joanne woke up, we began cutting up pictures of boys and girls and posting them into scrapbooks. 'They're *children*,' I said, and wrote *children* at the top of the page.

We made a flower page next. All the flowers were different. Some were big and some were small, some were red and some were blue, but they were all called *flowers*.

Ideas fought for position in my mind as enthusiasm took me in its grip. We could make pages of dogs, and trees, furniture, people

. . . we were all *people*. I was a person, Mick was a person. But Mick was also a parent, a man, an adult, a grown-up, an uncle, a friend, a husband. . . .

Before my mind could take me further, the door opened and Mick walked in. 'Sarah. Joanne,' I said. 'Here's my *husband* now. Hello *husband*.'

Mick smiled, thinking I was joking, when I was deadly serious. 'Hiya you two,' he said to Sarah and Joanne as they ran to him leaving the auditory training units blasting. I turned them off.

'Mick,' I shouted over Sarah and Joanne's voices. 'Sarah's trying to tell you about Simon down the road. She hasn't stopped asking about him since she found out he ran away from school this morning.'

Sarah had been so insistent on my repeating the story that I had capitalized on the opportunity and embellished it to such an extent, poor Simon was quite beyond redemption.

'Will you ask her what he's been doing?'

'What about Simon then?' Mick demanded of Sarah, putting his hands on his hips and feigning anger. 'What *has* he been doing?'

Sarah crossed her legs and folded her arms. Then she changed positions so her elbow was on the table, and her chin rested on her hand in true conversational style. She nodded for me to begin.

Little by little I related the story to Mick in such a way that Sarah could follow. Mick was brilliant. He drew breaths at exactly the right moments, shook his head in all the proper places, and smacked his leg to demonstrate what he thought Simon deserved.

Sarah copied his every move, and each expression on his face, loving every minute of it. She kept nodding her head as if to say, 'It's true Dad, really true.'

During the afternoon I had tried to make up for my lack of understanding by pointing to: boys fighting, a child running away from her mother, a girl stepping off the pavement without looking . . . and saying they were 'naughty'.

As for Sarah, she labelled every child she saw as 'gauky' and by the look on her face, it was one of the most comforting words she had ever learned.

'Sarah, find the *jam* in the cupboard please.' Sarah made no attempt to move. Without gestural clues she was often flummoxed by words I hadn't repeated enough times. I pointed to the cupboard. 'In the *cupboard*.'

'Joanne hasn't been well again Mick,' I said, turning to him. 'When I went to get her out of bed this afternoon she wouldn't stand up and she was really pale. Sarah. Sarah. Good girl. That's the *jam*. It's nearly *empty*.'

'Empee.'

'Yes, nearly *empty*.' I ran my finger up the outside of the jar and shook my head. 'It's not *full*.' I held up another jar. 'This is full.' I held up the jam-jar again, running my finger to the bottom of it. 'It's *not* empty.' I held up the jam-jar again and ran my finger almost to the bottom. 'It's *nearly* empty.'

'Maybe it's her teeth again,' Mick said, as he lifted Joanne on to his knee. She put her arms round his neck and, fixing her eyes on his, she blocked me from his view, presumably thinking that if he couldn't see me, he couldn't lipread what I had to say.

'I wonder if it's migraine. She slept practically all afternoon.'

'She ought to see the doctor again.' Mick put Joanne on the floor and, yawning, he went into the hall.

'Will you tell them about the television while I get the tea ready?' I called after him.

'I've just this minute walked in from school,' he replied. 'I've been working all day.'

'What do you think I've been doing?' My voice was hoarse from talking and my head ached from thinking what to say next.

'Let them watch the television if that's what they want to do.' Mick came back into the kitchen.

'What good is that? They won't get anything from it. Don't you want them to learn to talk?' It was out before I could check myself. I slammed a cupboard door.

'Here we go again. The same old story. Well I don't want to hear it.' Mick went into the lounge shutting the door behind him.

'Can't you think of something more original to say,' I shouted after him, before slamming three more cupboard doors, then one more for good measure.

During tea Sarah spat scrambled eggs on the tablecloth. It was her way of saying she didn't like eggs. She didn't like the banana either so she pulled a face and dropped it on the floor. She drank tea from her cup and let the liquid dribble down her chin because she was in one of those moods. She kicked Joanne because Joanne had accidentally touched her leg. When there wasn't anything else to do, she was bored, so she slid down her chair and went under the table.

I pulled her up again. 'Sit there until we've all finished tea.'

Sarah screeched and flapped her hands in the air, rocking the table and slopping tea into the saucers.

'Sarah stop making that noise. Be quiet!'

The tension was rising in me and there was an ache across my shoulders. Sarah ruined every tea-time. What if she always behaved like this? She had got to learn how to behave properly.

Sarah slid down from her seat again and pulled at the tablecloth. If she had been Joanne's age I might have tolerated such behaviour, but Sarah was nearly four. I looked at Mick. He was eating with a studied, controlled expression on his face.

I got hold of Sarah and dragged her out from under the table as she kicked and struggled. I pressed her into her seat and her hand caught one of the plates and sent it flying.

'Ignore her,' Mick said. 'Act as if she wasn't there.'

'But she has to learn how to behave at the table. We'll end up with a child we can't take anywhere.'

Sarah bit a piece of toast, then spat it out of her mouth.

'Stop spitting! You mustn't spit. Daddy doesn't spit. I don't spit. Eat your toast.'

Sarah chewed on her toast noisily.

Keeping within her view I said to Joanne. 'Joanne, can you eat quietly?' and I showed her.

Joanne took a biscuit from the dish and Sarah snatched it from her. Joanne stood on her chair to reach the biscuit and her hand went in the butter. I sat her down, wiped her hand, and, taking the biscuit from Sarah, gave it back to Joanne. I picked up another biscuit. 'Here's *your* biscuit Sarah. Watch how Daddy takes it from me. He doesn't *snatch*.'

I passed the biscuit to Mick, he took it from me, Sarah snatched the biscuit from him. As she sat down, she rocked the table again, and her elbow knocked over a cup of tea.

It was the final straw. I stood up shaking with anger. 'What are we supposed to do? Just let this happen? If you don't do something about her Mick I'll –' Words failed me.

Mick also stood up, slamming his knife and fork on the table at the same time – and I think even I was frightened. 'I've never known anything like this in my life. It's the same night after night.'

He leaned across the table and pulling Sarah from her chair, he hoisted her over his shoulder. 'You're going to learn once and for all my girl,' he said, as if he really thought he could teach Sarah anything 'once and for all'.

I made myself stay in the kitchen as Mick took Sarah upstairs, but after a few moments of listening to her screams, I couldn't bear it any longer and moved to follow them.

Mick was in Sarah's room and at first glance it seemed as if all hell had been let loose. Toys and clothes were strewn over the floor and one of the curtains had come away from the rail. The bed was ruffled and the wastepaper-bin was on its side, Sarah's crumpled drawings spilling from it.

There were excruciating screams coming from Sarah's direction as Mick tried to free himself from her clutches, but no matter what he did, he couldn't loosen her grasp on his sweater.

'Sarah, you're going to stay here until you learn,' he was saying. 'Let go!' Her hearing-aid was whistling, a shrill, monotonous sound.

In desperation Mick picked Sarah up, ran with her across the room, put her on the bed and then, tearing his sweater from her fingers, ran for the door. He reached it a moment before she did, and pulling it behind him, he knelt on the floor holding on to the door knob. His face was pale and his expression set. Nothing like this had happened to him before. Nothing was as Mick had expected it would be.

Sarah was tugging at the door-knob from the other side. When she finally accepted the door wasn't going to be opened, the tone in her screams changed and she began banging the wood with her fists. When it still didn't open she started throwing things round the room in a frenzy.

'Let me go into her Mick,' I said. 'She'll fling herself through the window in this mood.' Sarah was beyond reasonable thought and liable to do herself an injury.

'No one's going in. Leave this to me.'

We knelt on the floor waiting for Sarah's tantrum to subside and I pictured her every move by the sounds coming from the room. Ten minutes passed, though it seemed longer, and the screaming stopped. When we heard sobbing, Mick opened the door.

Sarah had her back to Mick as he entered the room, but she sensed his presence and whirled round. She was sobbing, her shoes were off, her hair was messed, her eyes were swollen with crying, her cheeks were a bright blotchy pink, yet she looked straight at Mick, walked up to him and coolly . . . kicked him on the shin.

'Right Sarah. You'll stay here until you learn.'

Mick had shut the door before Sarah recognized what he was going to do, then she ran to it, and what followed must surely have been a barrage of insults.

I knelt on the floor again, my stomach in a knot. I didn't want this. Why couldn't we be happy? Meanwhile Joanne, forgotten in the upset, had finished her tea and come upstairs. She stood beside me, her head level with mine, and her arm round my shoulder. And we waited.

Each time the room went quiet, Mick opened the door and went up to Sarah – and each time she kicked him on the shin. She was completely without fear and repentance was a word unknown to her. When she eventually gave in to the extent of not kicking, Mick held the door open for her to leave the room. As she came into the hall, her hands were on her hips and her head was high despite the sobs shuddering through her.

I put her nightdress on before carrying her down to the lounge where Mick was sitting. When I put Sarah on his knee, he held her close to him saying, 'Oh Sarah,' and he was clearly upset.

Why, oh why, did she do it?

I heard Joanne making little whimpering noises behind me and turned to see her rubbing her stomach. 'Bummy tore,' she said, and burst into tears.

Kneeling in front of her I said, 'Joanne is your tummy sore? Is it hurting?'

She nodded, and I hugged her to me, suddenly seeing how much she was being affected by all this. She didn't understand. All she saw was Sarah crying, and Sarah was her sister. It was even worse for her standing on the sidelines watching.

Mick held Sarah. I held Joanne.

God what a mess.

'Come with me Jo,' I said after a moment. 'We'll make some hot milk and you can give Sarah a biscuit.'

When the milk was ready, we took it into the lounge and Sarah's spirits revived. It was almost as if she had already forgotten the incident. She was cuddled into Mick's lap sucking her 'bit of stuff' – not the Sarah of upstairs, the real Sarah. We had reached her. But at what cost?

Feelings though were something I had been trying to help Sarah to have for a long time. I knew I had to pierce the seemingly impenetrable shell she had built around herself. I had tried to make it even clearer than I had before that I cared for her and loved her. Each night I chased her round the room for a kiss and insisted she sit upon my knee, and each night she arched her back, violently resenting the intrusion upon herself. She spat, kicked and butted me, until I put her down. But I always hugged her first and said, 'I love you Sarah.'

The routine was the same every day. It had to be, there was a lot to lose. If I didn't reach her now, I might never. She might grow and the protective shell grow with her as a shield to the world and everyone in it.

'I've got to go.' Mick had started to get up from his chair. 'I'm late for the match now, not that I feel like playing any more.'

'Just one more minute please.' There were some things I couldn't do alone.

'Sarah watch,' I said, putting my arms round Mick's shoulders. '*I* love Daddy.' I went over to Joanne and put my arms round her. '*I* love Joanne.' I went to Sarah and, kneeling in front of her, put my arms round her. 'Sarah. *I* love you too.' I held her tight. 'I love *you*.'

Sarah sucked her finger and assumed total ignorance. But I was sure she knew what I meant and that she was loved. Now I had to help her love others.

I took Sarah's 'bit of stuff' from her hand and, lifting her arms, put them round Mick's neck. 'Sarah. *You* love Daddy.' I called Joanne to me to sit her on Mick's knee as well. I lifted Sarah's arms again. '*You* love Joanne.'

The situation was contrived and there was no spontaneity, but it was the only way I knew how to help Sarah. When she was eventually to use the word 'love' it was a gesture only, with no such feeling behind it. One day, with practice, Sarah would learn what it is to love, and then perhaps, she would love me.

Mick went to play squash, I put Sarah and Joanne to bed and, after tidying the house, went to bed also. I needed to conserve my energy for the day ahead. Before I fell asleep I remembered that I hadn't told Mick about what happened in the sweetshop with Sarah and, in one moment of clarity, I saw what it had been like for him coming home from school. As I drifted into unconsciousness I realized I had considered everyone's feelings today, except his.

I woke in the early hours of the morning in a blind panic. My heart was thumping so hard I thought it might burst from my chest. Waves surged through my body and I fought against the feeling that I was going to faint. I closed the bedroom door behind me and paced the hall holding my throat trying to understand what was happening to me.

I was going to stop breathing. I ran to the bathroom and poured myself a drink of water, but, when I tried to take a sip, I couldn't swallow it.

There was an obstruction in my throat. A lump!

I leant against the basin wrestling with fear.

11. *Real tears falling*

The doctor could find nothing physically wrong with me. 'Perhaps I could do with a holiday,' I said to Mick.

'We only came back from your parents last week.'

'I know, but I still work when I'm there.'

'You take everything to excess.'

'I don't think you have the slightest inkling of what deafness really means,' I countered angrily. 'You can't just close your eyes and hope that everything will turn out all right.'

Immediately I said it I was sorry. There would be another argument. Mick would walk out. I had caused it again. It was as if I spent my whole life fighting. Fighting Mick, fighting Sarah, fighting every other person who stood in the way of what I was trying to do.

It was no use us talking now. It had gone too far for that. When we did the months of suppressed anger and resentment spilled, and we ended up blaming ourselves and each other for everything that was wrong in our relationship.

After Mick had left the house, I stormed into the lounge carrying toy bricks and chocolate drops to hide round the room.

When I was ready, I said to Sarah. 'Find the brick *behind* the chair.' I didn't use gesture with her because I wanted her to work out what the words meant for herself.

Gesturing reduced the need for thinking.

Sarah petulantly turned away.

'Joanne can you find the brick *behind* the chair then?' Joanne, tossing her shoulder-length hair, ran to the chair and bent to look underneath it.

'No Joanne. *Behind* the chair.'

The tone of my voice must have given her a clue, either that or she sensed my meaning, because she went behind the chair and held up the brick.

'Good girl. Your turn now Sarah. The brick is *underneath* the cushion.'

Sarah pretended she hadn't lipread me and waited for me to give her some kind of clue. But I wanted Sarah to think, and she hated having to think. Ease of thinking needed ease of language, something Sarah didn't have at her disposal.

I had to help her. 'Not on *top*.' I raised my hand. *'Underneath.'* I held one hand out flat with the palm upwards and my other hand below it.

Sarah threw the brick to the floor.

I heard Mick coming in and went into the hall to meet him. 'Mick will you try a lesson? Sarah might listen to you,' I said, ignoring the tension between us.

'With them! Both?'

Ever since Joanne's diagnosis, Mick had taken her for a lesson each night but had been unable to consider the prospect of a lesson with Sarah. He saw Sarah as my responsibility.

'Get the stuff out,' he said, after a considerable pause.

I put the doll's house on a stool and the auditory training unit on the floor on either side. I sat Sarah and Joanne down, fitted the earphones, then passed Mick the microphones. Sarah and Joanne were unexpectedly cooperative as they exchanged wry smiles.

Mick looked uncomfortable. The microphones were twisted round his neck, he couldn't stretch his legs, the floor was not where he usually sat, and he held a bag containing *doll's* furniture.

It couldn't have been easy for him. 'Will you give them some instructions?' I asked.

'All right, I know what to do,' Mick said impatiently, angry with me for getting him into this position.

'Oh and words like "on top, behind, in between . . ."' I added.

Mick lifted the doll out of the bag and held it near his mouth. 'Sarah. Put the doll *on* the bed. She can go to sleep.'

Sarah didn't move. Joanne suppressed a giggle.

Mick tried again. 'Sarah put the doll *on* the bed . . . All right if you don't want to play. Joanne. What have I got here?'

'Ewerweeon,' Joanne shouted, stretching her arms in the air.

'Good girl. It's the *television*. Put the –'

Sarah had reached forward and taken a sweet from the packet on the floor beside Mick. It was in her mouth before he could stop her. She looked at him without blinking, giving him her undivided attention. I knew she was planning her next move.

Mick persevered, refusing to give in, but the effort to keep Sarah and Joanne's attention on him caused perspiration to dot his forehead. I was surprised he continued because Sarah fidgeted, looked away, played with her socks, distracted Joanne, and yawned with slow deliberation, her timing perfect. Not only did she know how to infuriate, she also knew when her actions would have their most potent effect. Doing a lesson with Sarah was like going on a ten-mile run. It either left you weak, limp, and totally drained, which was usually the case, or with a wonderful sense of achievement.

Joanne leaned forward to touch the light-switch inside the doll's house, and Sarah pushed her hand away chanting 'Goaa gauky curl.'

She pressed the light-switch herself and when the light didn't come on, she crawled round to the back of the house to see why it wasn't working. The earphones were pulled from her head and a loud whistle ensued. Mick dragged her back by the legs. Sarah squealed and hit Joanne. Joanne hit her back.

'Give me patience,' Mick said, between clenched teeth.

Sarah reached for a sweet but Mick put the packet in his pocket. 'You're not having one. You don't deserve it.'

Sarah began screaming.

I intervened. The lesson had ended in chaos yet the opportunity had arisen for me to introduce a new idea. 'Sarah listen.' I held her arms. 'You're *angry*.' I motioned a churning in my stomach. 'You're *angry* inside.'

Her turmoil would have no release until she could describe that feeling for herself.

There was a glass of orange on the coffee table. I went over to it and knocked the glass over. 'Oh no!' I shouted as if in a temper. 'Sarah, I've spilt the orange juice. I'm *angry*.' She had to know that anger wasn't for her alone. Perhaps when she could say, 'I'm angry,' she wouldn't need to scream.

'Let's watch Lassie on television,' I suggested, and both Sarah and Joanne ran to the settee without me having to repeat myself once. While Mick cleared up the toys, I sat opposite them.

'Lassie has some puppies,' I said, as they appeared on the screen. 'They're her babies. *Puppies*. Look at them playing. They're having *fun*.'

'Aaah.' Sarah gazed at them wistfully, and rocked as if they were in her arms.

As the story unfolded, I tried to mime the feelings which mirrored my words. 'Lassie has lost her puppies. They've gone.' I mimed 'searching'. 'They've run a long way away.' I pointed into the distance and then 'ran' my fingers through the air. 'Lassie thinks', I pointed to my temple, 'she'll never see them again. No more puppies.' I let my shoulders drop and Joanne copied me, a mournful expression on her face. 'Lassie is *feeling sad* inside.' I pointed to my chest and looked 'sad'.

Over and over again I wrung Sarah's heart until she cried. Not crocodile tears, pretending. Real tears, hurting. Mercilessly I used her empathy with Lassie to strike chords within herself. So she would know what was meant by the words 'sad' or 'lonely' or 'unhappy' or 'happy', for only then could she give such feelings a place in her heart.

Lassie was to give me a parallel by which to work and I did so every chance there was. At the zoo the following week, Sarah cried when Mick told her the gorilla had toothache and wouldn't move from his cage until he had explained how the gorilla's pain would be eased. When at last she allowed us to move on, Joanne's knees buckled and she fell over.

'Sarah. Joanne's hurt,' I said, 'just like the gorilla. His tooth *hurt* him.'

If Sarah could 'feel' for a gorilla, then surely she could learn to 'feel' for Joanne.

Sarah ran to Joanne and patted her with feigned concern, when she turned away there was a smile on her face.

It would take time – but she would care.

Working through the emotions and all shades of them – kindness and unkindness, caring and uncaring, like and dislike – would take years. When I gave Sarah the word 'hate' it was alarming to see the vehemence with which she used the word. 'Hate liver, hate Goaa, hate socks, hate peas, hate water, hate you!'

Then I worked at modifying the feeling with 'don't like'. And soon Sarah didn't 'hate' the world, she just 'didn't like' it.

But I suppose that *was* an improvement.

12. *Once upon a time*

'Once upon a time there were three children who lived in London. . . .'

My spirits plunged. How could I tell Sarah the story of *Peter Pan* when she couldn't even understand the first sentence? I looked towards the books lining the shelves. Books filled with endless sentences. Millions of words. And panic gripped me. Sarah was starting school in four months. Time was running out.

It was Sarah's fourth birthday and for the past three weeks I had wanted to be like other mothers and to share in the mounting excitement as the big day approached. In our house birthdays and Christmas's only happened as the presents were unwrapped. I couldn't say: 'Sarah it's your birthday soon. We'll have jelly and a cake.' Sarah's reality was of the here and now, not 'in a while' and 'soon'.

Peter Pan was one of Sarah's gifts, and, once Mick had left for work, I lifted Sarah and Joanne on to my lap so that we could look at the story together. As pale pink pictures of cherubic children stared up at me, memories of my own intense pleasure in the story returned, and I longed to share this with them.

'That's a boy called Peter Pan and . . .'

Sarah and Joanne wriggled down from my knee leaving me to turn to the first page and the first sentence: 'Once upon a time there were three children who lived in London.'

In the following days I couldn't free myself from that sentence. Perhaps if I started to teach it it would be a beginning to all the other books. But how to start? Because their speech gave no indication of the actual depth to their knowledge, I couldn't even calculate the progress Sarah and Joanne were making.

Some time ago I had started setting myself small goals as it was hard to find motivation when the work seemed never-ending. I pinned a list of words to the back of the lounge door but a friend said she thought the words were too difficult.

I looked at the list. 'Automatic' was at the top. Had Sarah and Joanne been hearing children, they would have met the sort of words on the list all around them. In stories, conversation, and on the television. I believed that even if the words had little meaning for them now, they would still be stored in the recesses of their memories until I reintroduced them at a later date.

Even a word like 'transparent' could be introduced if it was followed with a simple explanation like, 'I can see through it'. Besides, I had found all the words on the lists in children's books, words such as 'precipice, fragile, delicious' and 'trespassing'. It was just as easy for Sarah and Joanne to learn the word 'delicious' for instance, as it was for them to learn 'nice', and infinitely more satisfying.

But making lists did not solve the problem of how I was going to introduce that sentence, 'Once upon a time there were three children who lived in London'. I decided that as Sarah and Joanne knew what 'children' meant, I would start with 'three'.

'Count my fingers,' I said. 'One, two, *three*. Here are *three* buttons. Count them with me. One . . .'

'Waa.' Sarah held up one finger.

'Do.' Joanne held up four fingers, then covered two with her other hand.

'*Three*,' I said.

'Go koo gay.' Saray deftly changed the subject.

'No, there's no *school* today.'

'Gaggy fooba.' Joanne kicked her foot in explanation.

'Daddy's not playing football. He's at work.' I went to the window. 'Look. Can you see the birds in the trees?'

They came to look and I said, 'Birds *live* in trees. Where does Mandy *live*? I pointed to her house. 'Mandy *lives* there. She lives in a house.'

We followed this with picture cards. We put the snail in its shell and the bee in the hive. 'The snail *lives* in his shell. The bee *lives* in a hive,' I told them and we all trooped outside to look for a snail.

It rained in the afternoon but this didn't stop us going in search of a 'village'. I had drawn pictures of a village before we left and there was an anticipatory air in the car as Sarah and Joanne competed to be the first to spot one.

'Dere,' Joanne shouted, as she pointed to the tops of houses showing above the trees.

A village however is smaller than a town. A town has more shops and offices. We went to our nearest town.

But a town isn't as big as a city. A city had a cathedral, and many more shops, offices, houses and factories. We went to stay with Jimmy and Barbara, friends of ours, who lived in a city called *London*.

I felt excessively pleased with myself. It had taken eight weeks and we had got as far as, 'There were three children who lived in London'. All I had to do now was to give Sarah the idea of 'Once upon a time'. It didn't matter for Joanne yet but it did for Sarah. Sarah hadn't a concept of time though. Her past was locked away without words to recall it. She couldn't say what she had done 'yesterday', 'last week', 'a year ago'. Even teaching 'in a minute' wasn't easy.

'In a minute Sarah.' I held up my finger to indicate that she must wait.

The car passed and we crossed the road.

'In a minute Sarah. You can have your biscuit, in a *minute*.'

Sarah held my hand while I ran up and down the hall with her until a minute had passed. Then I gave her a biscuit.

'In a minute' were wondrous words and they changed everything. Sarah no longer had to wait for some indeterminate length of time, perhaps for ever, when it was *now* that she wanted something more than she could bear. It was strange. I had held up my finger for as many months as I could remember and Sarah knew it meant 'wait'. Now it seemed as if the words gave my meaning definition, another dimension. Sarah's tantrums lessened, and we looked at each other with new understanding. And Sarah waited. It was only a *minute*.

A minute did not recall a past though. How could I help Sarah to have a past?

'You could try introducing the word 'before' into your conversation,' Miss Ayling suggested.

Early next morning I went into Sarah's bedroom and sat on her bed. When she opened her eyes and saw me, she smiled, and it seemed her blue eyes saw everything clearly, more clearly than I. In that silent world of hers there was a special knowledge and understanding. A wisdom greater than words.

'Sarah, here put your hearing-aid on. Good girl.'

'Eeeee-aye bhaa.'

'Your hearing-aid isn't broken.' I tickled her and she giggled. 'You're teasing me. . . . Listen. *Before* you went to bed,' I closed my eyes and rested my head on my hands, 'you had hot milk and a biscuit. You had a biscuit *before*.' I looped my finger to the left.

Sarah looked at me without any idea of what I was saying. I said it again and again.

When breakfast was over we went to the shops and on our return, I said, 'Sarah we went to the shops *before*. We bought some bread *before*. I looped my finger to the left, moving my head in the same direction.

Sarah was patient with me at first. Then impatient.

I gave her a sweet and waited ten minutes to say, 'You had a sweet *before*.'

Sarah crossed her arms as if to resist my words and, if that was not enough, crossed her legs too.

I tried to reach her, to forge a link between her mind and mine, but for a long time the chasm was unbridgeable. With each 'before' though, we came nearer, until one day it was no longer a concept adrift in the thing that's called time.

When Sarah said 'fore' we moved on. 'We went to the swimming baths before. *Yesterday* we went to the swimming baths.'

'A long time ago, not yesterday, *a long time ago*, we went to London. Do you remember?' I pointed to my head. 'That was *a long time ago*.'

Now Sarah could recall the past, the future would be easier. I looped my finger to the left, then 'rubbed' my hand as if to erase the sign. 'Not before,' I looped my finger in the opposite direction, '*after*. You can have ice-cream *after* your dinner.

'After your bed, *tomorrow*,' I rested my head on my hands and looped my finger to the right, 'we'll go to Grandma's'.

'Not *tomorrow*,' I looped my finger to the right and shook my head, '*in a long time*,' I looped my finger to the right several times, 'you will be five'. I held up one, two, three, four, five fingers. 'It will be your birthday *in a long time*.'

In this way Sarah's blinkered view widened until 'time' lay all around. It was a great relief to her to have a means whereby events could be neatly filed in her mind. Now she could recall with accuracy and plan with contentment. She had grasped one of the most difficult concepts to face any child, one which many deaf children never fully comprehend.

And, from a complexity of images, Sarah found order – and with order came peace.

One memorable day I lifted Sarah and Joanne on to the settee and opened the book of Peter Pan again. 'Listen to this story,' I said.

'*Once upon a time* there were three children who lived in London.

Their names were Wendy, Michael and John. They lived in an *enormous* house with an attic, a room under the roof. Their parents were called Mr and Mrs Darling. Daddy and I are called Mr and Mrs Robinson. They had a dog called Nana, and she was a special dog. There weren't many dogs like her, she did *special* things. She looked after the children and gave them a spoonful of medicine every single night – Monday, Tuesday . . .'

'Uggh.' Sarah pulled a face when I showed her the picture. 'I doh li mediee.'

'The children all loved Nana but she was very strict.'

Joanne copied my frown.

'One night when it was extremely dark – very very dark, a boy called Peter Pan came to London. Peter Pan was an *orphan*, he had no Mummy or Daddy. He fell out of his pram when he was a baby.'

Sarah's eyes were as wide as saucers, and Joanne looked as if she was trying to work this out in her head.

'Peter Pan could fly, and he flew to London to find his *shadow*. He had lost it.'

I got up and stood in front of the window so that my shadow fell across the floor. 'His *shadow*.'

'I do id doo.' Joanne scrambled down from the settee, falling on the floor in her haste.

Shadows take *time* and it was another ten minutes before we sat down again.

'When he got to the house someone barked loudly . . .'

'Gaga.'

'Yes it was Nana. . . . What a *lovely* story this is.'

13. *In a thousand different ways*

'You have some visitors,' I said. 'They're young. Female . . .
They're two girls called –'

'Manny, Chelle,' Joanne shouted, a smile crossing her face.

Mandy, and our other small neighbour Michelle, joined us
almost every day. They took part in our lessons and in any games
we were playing. Like Joanne, they thought our house a permanent
playground and I lured them shamelessly with toys, orange-juice
and cakes. Their presence, while not easing the struggle with
Sarah, allowed me to take her further than would have been
possible without them. Sarah still looked unutterably bored, but
she stayed seated merely because Mandy and Michelle did.

Mandy had gaps in her teeth and her thick brown hair was tied
back in a pigtail. Her fringe was cut in a straight line and she was
wearing striped trousers. Michelle had blonde, unmanageably fine
hair, fair skin, and an outgoing personality.

It was through Sarah's deep need for their friendship that I was
able to show her the rules which she must learn; the sharing, the
taking-turns, the giving and the receiving. Sarah was moody,
bad-tempered, a cheat. If she didn't win every game she would
ruffle the cards or toss the board in the air. We carried on without
her while she sulked, but each day she joined us a little bit more. In
small steps she conceded to our ways.

'Shall we play mothers or fathers, doctors or nurses?' I asked the
four children standing before me.

'Play liyar famiee,' Joanne tugged at my skirt. Her hair had lost
its curl and was cut in a shorter style. She was slender now – though
her appetite hadn't diminished along with the fat – and bronzed
from the hot summer. She still had a tendency to fall down, she
wore plasters almost permanently, but in trying to keep up with the
bigger children, her balance had improved.

When she spoke, and she never stopped, her sentences were full
of 'dis' and 'dat' and 'dere'. Her voice was sweet and clear, her

speech half baby-talk, half intelligible words. She could follow a story and, with help, make up a story, and though she couldn't pronounce everything properly, she still included words like 'automatic', 'supported', 'jealous', and 'drowning', in the right context. If I told her a story she seemed to understand the characters' every thought and action. She was like this in life too, perceptive, sensitive to people's feelings, and understanding.

'That's good,' I continued. 'We could pretend to be lions. Sarah, do you want to *pretend* to be a lion? It was Joanne's idea. She thought of it . . . in her head,' I added.

'Go.'

'Do you want to pretend to be a tiger with stripes then?'

Sarah's lips curled slowly as I rolled on the floor, behaving in the way I thought a tiger might. I would have done anything to take her from her black-and-white reality to a place where the colours of the imagination bloomed.

Seeing Sarah's cynicism, I didn't pursue the subject; instead I fetched blankets and sheets and, after draping them over the furniture, we got down on our knees. Everyone that is, except Sarah.

'Bummy qui liyar comin,' Joanne shouted excitedly.

'The lion's coming is he?' I raised my binoculars, two toilet-roll holders, and looked into the distance.

Sarah just couldn't hide her disdain. To her two toilet-roll holders were two toilet-roll holders, and blankets were blankets, not tents.

An hour passed. Mandy and Michelle went home for lunch, and I rose from the floor to collect the blankets and to bring the table from the dining-room into the lounge to use as a shop counter.

'Shall we get some *groceries* now, bacon, sugar, soup, and then we can play shops?' I suggested. I tried to inject a note of enthusiasm into my voice when I couldn't think of anything I wanted to do less. I hated playing games.

'I be choplady.' Sarah pushed her way in front of Joanne, who promptly kicked her. I was filled with admiration at this. Joanne knew what it was to cross Sarah. She had the marks to prove it.

I forcibly restrained Sarah from seeking retribution, and her hands flew to my face. I grabbed her by the wrist, but not before some damage was done, and fell back on to the settee while she fought to do more.

She had the smacking she had been asking for for the past week, and later, a much subdued Sarah presented herself to me.

'Sarah you can be the shoplady first if you help to get some tins from the cupboard.'

'Go.'

'Well I'm not getting them. It's no use tapping your foot like that either. Joanne will be the shoplady first then because she is helping to get the game ready ...' Sarah had turned away from me ignoring my words, and I made a decision to change what I had said. 'Do you want a bar of chocolate Sarah?' I said the words loudly so she would know I had spoken, even if she couldn't understand the words.

'Joanne do you want some chocolate?'

When she nodded I went to the drawer and gave her some chocolate which she turned over in her hands wondering what she had done to deserve it.

Sarah looked towards me for her bar.

'I asked you Sarah. I said, "Sarah do you want some chocolate?" but you looked away.'

Sarah didn't say anything. She knew it was justified, and Sarah had a strong sense of justice. It was a rotten trick to play. But I had talked it over with Miss Ayling and this had been the only thing we could think of to make Sarah realize she mustn't ignore me.

Joanne had gone from the room and when she returned she had packets and tins in a shopping-bag, as well as a toy register.

'I be choplady.' Sarah's voice rose.

'No, you won't help.'

I knew I was risking the possibility of Sarah refusing to play the game and this was something I very much wanted her to do. Only by re-enacting what went on in life could certain behaviour be explained to her, and being a shoplady was the first step in understanding the sort of jobs people do.

There was another reason why I felt it important Sarah join in the game. I wanted her to 'imagine' being a shoplady. To me this was the beginning of everything. Using her imagination would allow Sarah to see things in a thousand different ways, in an endless stream of possibilities. It would be her inspiration and her motivation. It would take her to where she had never been before.

But, because Sarah wouldn't help, Joanne was going to be the shoplady first.

'Joanne,' I called. 'I'm Mrs Brown the shoplady and you're the customer round there.' I pointed to the other side of the table, and then you can copy me afterwards. Pretend that's the door.'

Joanne dutifully walked into the 'shop' and, after tapping on an imaginary door, she caught her foot under a cushion on the floor. 'Oh dea me,' she giggled, getting to her feet.

When her dignity was restored, I said, 'Good morning Mrs Smith. It's a nice day isn't it? I think it will rain this afternoon though. I must remember to get my washing off the line. What would you like to do today?' I asked, suddenly realizing that Joanne had never heard a conversation between a shopkeeper and a customer.

I removed the apron I was wearing, ran round the other side of the counter, donned a hat, and picked up a shopping-bag. 'Joanne, this is what you say . . . Good morning Mrs Brown. It is warm today. I'd like some soup please.'

I pulled the hat off, dropped the shopping-bag, and ran round the counter again. 'What did you want Mrs Smith?'

'I wan dom doup. . . .'

Sarah had snatched the hat from Joanne's head. Grandma's old one with the black ribbon and lace.

'No Sarah, it's your turn in a minute. In a minute!' As I spoke my heart began thumping and waves of panic swept over me. I broke into a hot sweat. I tried breathing deeply but it felt as if I was choking and my lungs were closing in. I took shallow breaths and moved nearer to the window. The lump was present all the time now. Some days my throat ached until my voice was hoarse and my neck swollen. I saw futility in all effort. Sarah and Joanne would grow and die, our lives were but seconds in time. I couldn't give in though, not yet. Joanne was nearly all right, but not Sarah. She needed me.

In time the panic subsided. I was almost in control again when Mick came in. 'Go and lie down,' he said.

'I can't. Miss Ayling's coming.'

'I'll do the lesson, you go to bed.'

I knew how much Mick would hate working with Sarah in front of Miss Ayling. He had begun taking her on his own now, though Sarah invariably kept him teetering on the edge of his nerves for the full fifteen minutes. But he had become closer to her because of it.

'Don't you ever do that to me again,' Mick commented when Miss Ayling had gone.

'Why what happened?' I asked laughing.

Mick perched on the edge of the bed. 'Well, I held up a picture of a lion. "Look," I said. "The lion has a tail." Then I picked up a picture of a monkey. "The monkey has a tail too. A dog has a tail and . . ."

' "What else has a tail Joanne?" Miss Ayling asked.

'Straightaway, Joanne got down from the table and began pulling at my trousers trying to undo the zip. "Daddy tail look." she was shouting, and it was the clearest I've ever heard her speak.'

'I thought Miss Ayling had cut short her visit,' I laughed. 'I feel better now. I think I'll get up.'

When I was dressed, I collected the overdue library books and, as I put them in the car, I heard the sound of a plane passing overhead. I looked up to see a trail of white vapour emblazoned across the sky. At that moment a young child's voice from behind me said, 'Daddy. What's that coming from the aeroplane?'

I turned round. The boy was at least two years younger than Sarah.

And she had never asked a question.

14.   *A daily routine*

Sarah had questioned in her own way, but had never actually *asked* one. She had so much knowledge stored in her head now. I could make her understand almost anything. But questions, they were different.

Before Miss Ayling had time to take off her coat the next time she came, I said, 'When will Sarah be able to ask a question?'

Miss Ayling carried on removing her coat. 'I'm thinking Kath. Let me have some time because I've got to find out about this.'

I was bursting with impatience. I couldn't see how this one could be solved. Sarah had never heard people question each other, and they rarely, if ever, questioned her. Even if she did one day learn to understand what a question was, and to answer it, how would she ever manage to turn the words round so she could ask the things *she* wanted to know, not the things that I, or anyone else for that matter, thought she ought to know.

Miss Ayling brought a book with her the following Monday. 'I've chosen this,' she said, 'because the pictures are self-explanatory.'

As she sat opposite Sarah, I lifted Joanne on to my knee. Joanne straightened her skirt and her hearing-aid whistled. I felt so tired and my body weighed me down. I had been hoping for some months that Sarah would be able to go to school after her fourth birthday. I didn't want her to go to a special school but I had tried to accept it as the Head had said it was the right place for her. When he had said she couldn't go until September, I didn't know what to do. Each day was like pushing myself through an endless peat bog.

Miss Ayling turned the pages of the book and held it up so that the picture faced Sarah. 'Ask a question then answer it yourself like this. Sarah. Where is the dog?'

'Gog gone.' Sarah turned the palm of her hands upwards, and tilted her head to explain she didn't know where the dog was. She hadn't needed to speak. Her expression could echo her thoughts and feelings, almost as if her thoughts and feelings had a face.

'Gog gone,' Sarah repeated. She looked round the room, then under the table. Laughing, she pointed to the picture. 'Gog in car.'

'Good girl. The dog is in the car,' Miss Ayling said.

Sarah would probably think that that was the way, the only way, to answer the question, 'Where is the dog?'

'What is the dog doing Sarah?' Miss Ayling waited a moment to give Sarah time to think of an answer, then she said, 'He's looking out of the window. Who is that?' She pointed to the boy in the picture.

'Dat's Pe-er,' Joanne said casually over the thumb in her mouth.'

'Yes, that's Peter. Sarah. *Who* is that? That's *Peter* isn't it?'

When Miss Ayling left I knew I must begin filling my days with questions. Questions which I must answer myself. I felt renewed energy. Knowing what to do was half the battle. It was not knowing what to do that caused all the worry.

I went to the kitchen drawer and got out some forks. '*Where* shall I put these?' I asked. 'I'll put them on the table.'

'What dat for?' Joanne asked, pointing to a mole on Sarah's neck.

'That's a *mole*. Look you have one too,' "Joanne's *mole*", I wrote on a card. "Sarah's *mole*", I wrote on another.

Reading had been introduced into our house ever since I had read an article entitled 'Bombard them with the written word'. This article had a photograph of a family at breakfast with the mother holding up a flashcard saying, 'Here is the *jam*.'

From that moment on our house had been labelled. 'This is the *television*.' '*Shut* the *door*.' '*Come in*.' '*Go out*.' '*Sit down*.' confronted our every move. At the time reading was low on my list of priorities for Sarah, and not on it at all for Joanne. Its importance in the long-term however couldn't be underestimated. Thinking would be easier for Sarah if she had a concrete visual image of words to support her elusive auditory one.

The day after I had read the article, Mick brought home a piece of wood to hold flashcards, and, at breakfast next morning, I placed it in front of me. I had laid the table carefully and placed cards against several items on it saying: 'Here is the *spoon*.' 'This is the *sugar*.'

Mick poured himself some cereal and seeing me fit a card into the wood said, 'Can you wait until I've eaten?'

'But they'll have finished their food by then.' Sarah listened at mealtimes when there was food to keep her occupied.

'Joanne.'

Joanne raised her head and I pointed to each word on the card. 'Please . . . pass . . . me . . . the . . . *butter.*' I asked Joanne first because Sarah needed time to be drawn into any kind of game.

Joanne looked round the cards on the table. Seeing the right one, she propelled it towards me. Sarah picked it up. A scuffle ensued.

'I'm just about to go to work,' Mick said. 'Can't we have a few minutes' quiet.'

'I don't want to do this either,' I said. 'I won't be long, I promise.' I put my finger to my lips. 'Shh Sarah. Right Joanne, say the words for me.'

'Pease,' she whispered.

'Please,' I repeated.

'Pad me de budder.'

'Very good girl. Your go now Sarah.' I placed another card in the wood which said, 'Please pass me the *salt.*'

Sarah looked round the cards on the table, and finding the right one, passed me the next one to it. Then she bent her head.

How could I get her to look at me again? I picked up the salt cellar and sprinkled salt on my toast.

Sarah lifted her head, a bemused expression on her face.

'That's a good thing to teach them,' Mick said.

I turned the wood round to face him. 'Daddy's turn now.'

Since that day reading became an accepted part of our daily routine. Now *questions* were to be part of it too.

15. *The visit*

As I turned the corner of the road and looked along the length of beach towards the expanse of sea, my sense of loneliness increased. Today Sarah and I were going to visit the School for the Deaf for the first time.

A few months ago, the mother of one small boy at the school said to me, 'Sarah will be signing in a week, just you wait and see. It always amazes me how quickly they pick it up.'

I met her words with a smile to hide the misery I felt. I had tried hard not to think of Sarah signing, or of her being with children who signed, because I was afraid it would work against everything we had tried to achieve. We were drawing her outwards, and into society. Wouldn't signing draw her inwards and away from it?

I must shut my eyes. Sarah was deaf, and signing may be a part of deafness in the way that a hearing-aid was a part of it too.

To me a special school held stigma; it hinted of failure, being second best, not as good as the rest.* But in acknowledging the presence of stigma, I was able to give it the importance it deserved. No importance at all.

Half an hour later I was edging the car into a narrow entrance by the side of a large blue sign saying, 'School for the Deaf and Partially Hearing'. Then another, 'Go slow'.

Around the corner were seventy deaf children who wouldn't hear my car.

In the car park the rear windows of the teachers' cars had bright yellow stickers which blazed the words, 'Mind that child, he may be deaf'.

This was a place for deaf people and I didn't belong. It was outside anything I had ever known before, yet it had been decided

* My views at this time on special schools (integration, communication methods, language teaching etc.) do not necessarily reflect views held now.

103

that Sarah should be here. It was like giving her up to a different
world.

'My koo,' Sarah said as she climbed out of the car and pointed to
the building.

I bent down and tidied her hair. 'You look nice. I love your *new*
dress.' It was purple cotton with a floral pinafore, and it had a
matching frill round the neck. 'This is your *new* school. You'll stay
here all day. All morning, have your dinner, all afternoon, after
dinner.'

I didn't know whether Sarah was looking forward to starting
school next week, because she gave no sign of her feelings. Outwardly, she was calm and accepting. I had the feeling Sarah
purposely concealed her emotions from me. It was her way of
retaining her power.

We waited in the entrance hall for the Head. Windows looked
out on to an inner courtyard filled with shrubs and tropical plants.
The sun shone brightly through the glass on to children's paintings
on the walls.

The paintings looked normal.

I heard a movement to my right and turned – a split second
before Sarah – as a door was opened by a child of about six. I
recognized the piercing whistle of a hearing-aid, only now there
were several whistles, even more piercing, coming from several
hearing-aids.

I heard voices too. Voices that seemed to come from the
beginning of time. I glimpsed machines, children with earphones. . . . Why? Why? Why? This wasn't Sarah. She wasn't deaf
like this.

The girl started walking towards us and I felt myself go hot and
cold. What would I say? She came to stand in front of me, looking
directly into my eyes. She began to speak, and her voice sounded
awkward and laboured. I didn't know what she was saying to me. I
smiled and nodded as if I understood her, because I wouldn't have
wanted her to know that I did not. I picked up the hem of her dress.
'I like your dress.'

She smiled and I began to relax. Her hair was a mass of tight
curls and though it was fair, her eyelashes were dark. She was quite
unselfconscious, not concerned with how she should behave, but
open and friendly in the way a much younger child might be.

She spoke again. Her voice was without inflexion or control. She
pointed to me questioningly. I noticed she directed her query to me
though it was Sarah's name she wanted. She had either taken it for

granted Sarah couldn't talk, or that she wouldn't understand her.

'That's Sarah,' I said really clearly.

She spoke again and her hand moved between us.

'Yes. I'm Sarah's Mummy.'

She pointed again, and held out her hand as if to measure the air.

'Sarah's my little girl.' I patted my chest and held my hand in the air too.

She nodded, apparently satisfied, and walked away, our conversation over. At the door of the classroom she turned to wave.

I heard another door open and footsteps coming down the hall. Fear raced through me. There was no going back. This school had to be faced.

The Head welcomed me, and had a special greeting for Sarah which made her blush. He had an international reputation for his work with parents of pre-school children. He said he had seen the most ordinary mums do the most extraordinary things. He believed it wasn't a mother's intelligence or education which brought results, but caring.

He led us down the corridor towards the Infant Department and on the way we passed more children's paintings, every one a life-size drawing of the children themselves. A black hearing-aid adorned each child's chest, and I thought of Sarah's self-portrait soon to hang there. She would draw her aid just as surely as she would her nose.

The large classroom seemed overcrowded when we entered, children milled around, not sitting at desks, but standing in pairs or small groups as four adults moved amongst them. In one brief moment the image of that classroom seemed to banish all hope for Sarah. There was no reason to suppose she could be different from any other child here.

And yet I saw children whose faces brimmed with mischief, and I heard laughter echoing. Yes, it was a happy atmosphere, and the staff would care.

After the Head had left, I watched the teachers as they worked with small groups, and the auxiliaries talking to the remaining children who were painting. The groupings were changed often, probably because the children's attention span, like Sarah's, was short.

Hearing-aids whistled incessantly and that, together with the bizarre noises the children were making, their grimaces and gestures and their movement around the room, gave an impression of disorder. But after a while it became obvious that the day was tightly scheduled, and the organization minutely planned.

The Head had introduced me to Sarah's new teacher. She was motherly and kind. She would be my substitute from now on and the main influence upon Sarah during the day. She was young and her hair was flecked with ginger. When she spoke to Sarah, Sarah understood her. One more person. When there were so few, each earned my undying gratitude.

'Would you like to watch a lesson Mrs Robinson?' the teacher enquired.

She collected five children and ushered them into a corner of the classroom which was separated by a wooden screen. The children, three boys and two girls of about five or six years of age, sat on small chairs in a semi-circle around her. Next to her was a group aid with several pairs of earphones and numerous controls.

'The advantage of this group aid', the teacher told me, 'is that besides being linked to me, the children can hear their own and each other's voices as well.'

I knew this to be the theory. In practice the children may have heard some sounds, but understanding what those sounds were through their hearing was another matter. Anyway the teacher's voice was the only intelligible voice amongst them.

It took a lot of encouragement from the teacher before the children were settled and listening to her. It must have been like sitting and watching someone speaking in a strange language without being able to hear the rhythm or the pattern of the words.

'One, two, three, four, five. Once I caught a fish alive. Six, seven, eight, nine, ten, then I let it go again.' The teacher mimed the actions to the rhyme.

One or two of the children opened and closed their mouths, copying her lip movements. A girl fiddled with the wires hanging from the earphones on her head. A boy stared at the teacher, a blank expression on his face. When he saw the child by his side copying the teacher's actions, he joined in. Every now and then he repeated a word, one step after the teacher had spoken. Paul, the youngest in the group, fidgeted in his seat and stared round the classroom.

It seemed a hopeless task as the teacher strove to bring the children's attention to her face. Maybe with one she had a chance, but five? all with varying degrees of understanding. And at least two of the children had yet to reach the stage of recognizing there were such things as words.

I imagined trying to teach five 'Sarahs' and the thought brought me out in a sweat. I knew the vast amounts of energy needed to keep one step ahead, yet the teacher did this for children who weren't even hers.

During the morning I talked to Sarah as much as I could. It had come as a sickening jolt to realize that in this school she could only receive a fraction of the language I could give her at home. Here, sixteen children clamoured for attention. The teachers might even cover ground we had covered many times before. I wanted the school to add to her knowledge, not repeat what she already knew. I didn't say anything though. I had to learn to take a back seat now.

But I wished I had kept Sarah at home longer.

Our presence had been signalled around the room yet none of the children approached us. At break-time though, they crowded round Sarah and asked me, in their way, for her name. Again they asked me, not Sarah.

When break had ended one of the children came with me for his medical examination. Sarah held my hand on one side, Peter held my hand on the other. Perhaps it was the way he came to me so trustingly which made me feel protective towards him. His glasses were of the old National Health sort, round and brown-rimmed, and they were held together by a grubby piece of sticking-plaster. His jumper was frayed at the edges and the grey wool pulled in many places. It seemed to me that in Peter lay the vulnerability of all deaf children. What chance for someone like him in this sophisticated world, tough to its very core?

Many of the other children had worn glasses. But lipreading was such an exact art. It was so unfair. So unjust. Sarah had good eyesight, intelligence, she was strong and healthy. Sarah for all her tantrums was secure. It was this that affected me more than anything. What was the future for the deaf children here?

'How many words can Sarah say?' asked the doctor.

I shrugged my shoulders. 'About a hundred I suppose.'

There was a silence. A hundred words didn't sound very many.

Apologetically, I added, 'But she probably understands about two thousand or more.'

The doctor was looking at me with a thoughtful expression. 'That's very good,' she said.

Why did she think it was good? I started to say something, then didn't. I said nothing.

A week later Sarah's name joined the ranks of the others in the school magazine. And Sarah brought home her first sign. An eloquent two fingers raised, and a practised flick of the wrist.

16.   The final stage

In the next five months Joanne's progress was astonishing. It was hard to believe that in the months following the diagnosis of her deafness she had done what other, hearing children take at least two or three years to do. Between the ages of twenty-two months and three years she had acquired a fundamental language, and between three years and three years five months, she had used that language to speak. She was also an able reader, and the foundations for every subject she would learn in school had been laid.

Undoubtedly she was bright. And she gained in the 'opportunity' for learning that had been presented to her, and the use she had made of it. Intelligence, like anything else, prospers in the right conditions. Thus her deafness had been turned into advantage. Had she been born a hearing child she would have received a similar opportunity for learning but nothing like to the same extent. Any child (slow-learning, deprived, handicapped, nonhandicapped . . .) would have progressed with the kind of stimulation Joanne was receiving each day.

By encouraging her language other aspects of her development benefited too: her general knowledge, her ability to concentrate, her memory. She was learning to think of others, be appreciative, and to make decisions. She was gaining a sense of morality and acquiring values. . . .

Miss Ayling's guidance was crucial to Joanne's progress, although Sarah helped too. It was through her that I had become skilful at helping to develop language in a child. In turn Joanne helped Sarah, for much of the work I did with her during the day I adapted for Sarah at night.

Working with Joanne, however, was never like working with Sarah. It was *work* to Sarah. It needn't have been, that was the sad part, for Sarah resisted learning because she was resisting us. It was as if she was saying, 'I must fight to survive'. Ironically, her very survival depended upon her learning.

To Joanne work was play. Everything was a game to her. I knew now what was meant by the words, 'Enjoy your child'. To have a conversation, an exchange of thoughts and ideas, was unimaginable delight. Now that Sarah was at school there was a hole in my day. I felt cut off from her, as if part of me were missing. There was the distance between school and home, and she couldn't bring her day home for us to share. When she walked out of the door until she returned, her time was a complete blank to us. But now I could concentrate on Joanne. We had a whole eighteen months together before she started school. It seemed like a lifetime.

Having deaf children had turned out to be something of an advantage for me. I had no alternative but to give language. In giving language I gave time. In giving time I gave myself. And that was all Sarah and Joanne really needed.

Some part of my day with Joanne was spent playing games. Any game was useful, or could be adapted to be useful in some way; remembering objects on a tray was good for memory, as were certain card games; drawing patterns developed pencil control, necessary for writing later on; putting objects in order, big, bigger, biggest, developed a concept of size, or it could be shape or colour; putting objects in sequential order developed the idea of working from left to right, a necessary concept for reading; feeling objects in a bag and describing them without saying what those objects were developed logical thinking and self-expression. In other words being able to say what you are *thinking*.

Lately, I had been concentrating on games which posed problems. Joanne loved solving problems. Sarah much preferred having her problems, the thinking ones at least, solved for her.

One morning I asked Joanne to choose a game from the cupboard and she brought a flat box to me. It was a game I often used to encourage her to 'think'.

'Right Jo. Choose a card. Describe it to me and I'll have to guess what it is.'

'It got a ball and a dog. The dog id kicking the ball.' Joanne tugged at the neck of her sweater, as if it were annoying her. I had tied her hair in pigtails and the ribbons were a matching colour. Though she missed Sarah, she enjoyed having me to herself, and our relationship was both companionable and fun.

I picked up a card. 'Listen carefully and picture it in your mind. It's got four wheels and it's for carrying something . . . It has a hood. You had one when you were little. *Think* about it.'

'I used to push it? It got four wheels?'

'No, I know what you mean. The baby walker. You're nearly right.'

'It was dat yellow ting.'

'No. This wasn't something you would have pushed. This is something you would have sat in.'

I didn't give Joanne any more clues because I wanted her to search her memory for an answer. I wanted her to link certain images in her brain. To think. Just as children need practice of speaking, they also need practice of thinking.

'A pram.'

'Good girl. Why did it have a hood do you think?'

'To keep de dun out.'

'I see. It was to *shade* the baby from the sun. What else?'

'De rain.'

'Did the baby need protecting from the rain?'

'So she couldn't get wet. I couldn't get wet.' Joanne changed the 'she' to an 'I'.

She picked up another card and, shielding it from me, said, 'It got a plant. It got some green tings. Um, what dat called?'

'That's a plant pot. You were describing a plant but you gave the game away. Now, how many more cards than you have I got?'

'You got one more. You got two more.'

'No look. I've got one more than you. You've got none at all. If I give you three cards.' I placed three cards in front of Joanne and two cards for myself.

'I got two more.'

'Listen. I have two cards and you have . . . ?'

'Three.'

'So how many more than *me* have you got?' I persevered with the question. 'More' and 'less' were the basis of addition and subtraction. Miss Ayling had shown me what to do.

'One more.'

'Good girl. Now shall we have a look at the photo album?'

When Joanne was sitting on my knee and the album was open, I pointed to the bridesmaid in the picture. 'You have a friend who has the same name as this bridesmaid here haven't you?'

Joanne crinkled her eyes and clasping her hands behind her head said, 'Vewonica my friend. She alway do funny tings.'

'You run about in the corridor with her after school is finished don't you?'

'Who de cowidor?'

'You know, outside the classroom.'

'Yes, Shaun is de peeceman. Shaun is a man and I tell to stop car.'

'Can you read this for me?'

Underneath the photos I had written short sentences. I did this with holiday snapshots, anything that was personal, and therefore meaningful, to Sarah and Joanne.

'Mummy-is-de-bride. Daddy-is-de-bridegroom,' Joanne read.

'Who do you think is marrying us?'

'De Pist.'

'And what does the *Pr*iest say?'

'Daddy will you be mudder's husband?'

Sarah couldn't have made up her own version of what the Priest might have said. She would either have repeated something I had told her previously, or said nothing at all. Joanne was *thinking* for herself.

'Are you going to get married one day do you think Joanne?'

'Yeh. When I growed up I going to marry Jeffrey 'cause he'd a nice boy.'

Joanne had many friends at nursery school, though how she managed there was beyond me. The hearing-aid she wore boosted all sound equally so the background noise, together with the children's immature speech, created an almost uniform sound, indistinguishable without intense concentration. How exhausting was it for Joanne, when she faced a major obstacle each time a child spoke?

It was different at home. The house was quiet and the rooms small. We spoke within Joanne's range of hearing, and we adjusted our speech to her level of understanding.

At ten to five the school bus honked its horn outside the house and we went to the door to welcome Sarah. As usual she presented us with a sullen face.

'Sarah you're not coming in like that. You make us very sad. You must learn to smile and say hello properly. Go outside and we'll try again.' And before Sarah had time to realize what was happening she was outside and the door was closed.

It was dark and Sarah was screaming. 'I've never heard any-thing like it,' Mick said. 'Let her in.'

'She's got to learn.' I had been working hard on Sarah's smile. It was important she look approachable and welcoming.

Eventually I was forced to open the door and Sarah stopped screaming. She walked past us into the hall and muttered a deep 'hello'. On her lips was a fixed and rigid grin.

My heart melted. 'Hello Sarah,' I said, putting my arms round her. 'What did you do today?'

Sarah loosened her tie, and resigned herself to politeness. 'Wen koo bud playmilk work had dinner word bud home.'

'Oh that was interesting.' I looked towards Joanne who was stifling an exaggerated yawn. Sarah said the same thing every day. It wasn't that she couldn't say more, she just chose not to.

'What did you have for dinner?' I asked, taking Sarah's coat from her.

Her reply was a two-word dismissal which, although having been lipread wrongly by her, and in turn lipread wrongly by the children who taught it to her, was abundantly clear to me.

I hung up her coat and pretended, not that I hadn't heard, but that I hadn't seen.

At the end of tea, Joanne put her head in her hands and murmured, 'Dank you God for my dinner. Abet,' then she stood up, placed one hand on her stomach, and with the other she traced a wide arc in the air to her forehead. 'Name Fader,' her hand leaped to her chest, 'and de Dun,' and moved on to her stomach, 'Holy Spitit, Abet.'

Joanne prayed anywhere, everywhere, and especially in the bathroom. With a book at her feet, knickers round her ankles, she showered 'Dear Cods' into the air and chanted glorious 'Hail Marys' until the rafters begged for mercy.

'Mummy id Cod deaf?'

'I don't know Joanne. Mind you if He was deaf where would He get his hearing-aid batteries from?'

Joanne giggled, hiccupped, and giggled again. 'Who made me?'

Joanne's questions caught me by surprise. Even though religion had a prominent position in our house, she wasn't even four yet. Religion had been very helpful to me. How else could I encourage Sarah, for instance, to develop a conscience: to know the difference between right and wrong? How does one develop this inner morality with someone like Sarah whose only thought was her own without regard for others? Religion helped me to give her reasons.

'God made you.'

Joanne considered this for a moment. 'If Cod made me, who made Cod?'

'God has always been there since the beginning of time. Always and always.'

Joanne nodded. 'When is His birthday?'

'I don't suppose He has one, otherwise He would be millions and millions of years old.'

'Cikey.'

'Crikey.'

'Where was I before I was born?'

'You were in heaven Jo.'

'I tink I wad lonely in heaven,' she said. It was so beautiful, yet inside me was a feeling that it couldn't last. I don't know why I should feel this way with Joanne, and not with Sarah. It was as though her hearing hung in the balance, held only by a thin spidery thread. Without doubt it was her most precious possession, that bit of hearing more than Sarah's. I was scared it would be taken from her, that it was only on loan for a short while. It had made me prepare her, just in case.

I had only a few months left with Joanne before she started school. Originally her name had been down for the Partial Hearing Unit – this was a specially equipped classroom within a hearing school – then it was decided that she should continue from the nursery into the infant class at her own school. I hadn't been happy about this as I knew she would only receive about half of what went on in class, but the Head of the School for the Deaf had said, 'If she can manage in a hearing school with hearing children, it will benefit her for life. One day if she can get through a comprehensive and cope, she will get through life.'

That evening I went into Sarah's room to find her sitting up in bed reading a comic. I lay beside her trying to work through the dense forest of my muddled thoughts. I felt like a blind person searching for a destination without knowing which way to go or how to get there, and with only my instinct to guide me. Yet this was the most important stage of Sarah's development.

I wanted Sarah to think for herself. All her life she had said my words and thought my thoughts. She was only what I allowed her to be. In 'thinking' lay Sarah's creativity and her individuality. Thinking would allow her to make decisions, reason, reflect, calculate, ponder on the past, draw on knowledge, create new ideas. . . .

Thinking would allow her to develop: who she thinks she is and what she thinks she would like to become.

If words are the tools by which we communicate our needs, feelings and ideas, it is through questions that our minds are freed to think.

Sarah understood certain questions now, such as 'What?'

'Where?' 'Do you know?' but others, 'How?' 'Why?' 'If?' only caused her annoyance.

Sarah was sucking her finger beside me and her 'bit of stuff' lay over my face. When she noticed this, she giggled and I tickled her. We had a game, then I opened a book.

'Why are the children going out Sarah?' I asked. 'Why do you *think*?'

. . .

'They're going out to buy some food. Look they have a shopping-bag with them.'

'What would happen if they forgot their money? What do *you* think would happen?'

. . .

My questions continued without answer.

'Sarah what would happen if I ate all the cakes? What do you think?'

Sarah stared at me – a wall between her mind and mine.

I tried to show her how to do it, that she must, from a range of possibilities, drawing on the experience of the past, *predict* what might happen in the future.

'I suppose I might get fat or . . .' I nodded for Sarah to speak.

. . .

'Or I might be sick . . .' I nodded again.

. . .

'Or it might spoil my teeth. Sarah what do you think will happen?'

'Bummy ged fad.'

You think I will get fat? I might get so fat I'd burst. Sarah, do you know where dinosaurs get their food?' Dinosaurs were her current favourite 'monster'. 'Do they get it from the ground or from other animals? Perhaps they eat fish.'

'No, the treed.'

'Good girl. They would get their food from the trees. And what do you think they would feel if a monster came? I wonder what they would feel?'

'Frighten. Runned away.'

'Good good girl. They would probably run away. I wonder where to? Perhaps a castle, the moon, a cave . . .'

I felt as if I was pushing my way into a resisting force. As though the pathways linking experience were rusty with ill-use or had simply never been formed. Whatever the answer, the effort it imposed upon Sarah was unlike anything she had known before. If

I could not go one way, I must go another. I diverted and forged my way through new territories, first one direction then the other. By all manner of converging pathways and triggered memories, we would arrive at a thought. This thought would be new. It would be Sarah's. With time and practice, all thoughts would make their connections with a fluency which did not for the moment exist.

'Sarah, what do you think you will have for your birthday?'

Sarah searched her memory to recall the word 'birthday' which would in turn unleash a host of other recollections.

'For your *last* birthday you had a handbag and a book about Peter Pan.'

Sarah nodded, suddenly remembering.

'So what do you think you will have for your birthday when you are five?'

'Cake.'

'*You* think you will have cake? *I* think you are right.'

Soon Sarah was asleep and I knew she wouldn't stir before morning. One night about a year ago, she had quite unexpectedly, gone straight to sleep and since then had never once woken during the night. The way she did it made me think she had come to a decision, and having made that decision, there was no going back on it.

I could hear Joanne singing and went into her bedroom where I was met with, 'Why didn't Jedud marry a deaf wife?'

'She probably didn't hear Him ask.'

Joanne buried her head in the pillow to smother her laughter. 'I wish I wadn't deaf Mummy,' she lifted her head. 'Would you like to be deaf?'

'Only if it meant I could be like you.'

'Mary id our mother. I've got two mothers. I'm glad you're my Mummy.'

'I'm glad I'm your Mummy too.'

When I left her, Joanne was lying on her back with her face turned in an upward direction mouthing her prayers.

She had obviously realized that if God was deaf He would need to lipread too!

Things had improved for me. One week after Sarah had started at the School for the Deaf, I went for a whole day without a panic attack. When the space between attacks was as long as a week, they ceased altogether. With their demise, the lump in my throat disappeared. So ended the worst eighteen months of my life.

17.   *What went wrong?*

I think, deep down, I had always known the School for the Deaf could not give Sarah any of the opportunities we wanted for her, nor the stimulation she was capable of utilizing. In my opinion Sarah was being held back.

The school had seventy pupils between four and sixteen, and their range of language was as wide-ranging as the number of children in the school.

The problems for learning were immense. There were senior children with less language than junior children, and severely deaf children with more language than partially hearing children, and children who had received an early diagnosis and pre-school help, who did not make the progress one would have expected of them, and others who did. There was no rule for one, nor one rule for all.

There were children with additional handicaps, maladjusted children, and children who had specific language problems quite apart from those caused by deafness.

Sarah was receiving language from specialist teachers, but only a fraction of the language which surrounds a hearing child each day. If Sarah was ever to catch up, before the gap became unbridgeable, she would need at least as much language as hearing children, not less.

She was progressing with reading, writing and arithmetic. Only I wasn't interested in these when Sarah couldn't talk to me.

But what else was there for her? Helplessly, I saw our evenings being spent doing work which could, in another situation, have been done during the day, leaving us free to give her the extra help she needed.

Each time I went into the school now it took days to shrug off my low spirits. How could I say Sarah could do better, without it sounding as if the staff weren't doing their job properly, or that the children were less able than Sarah, neither of which was true?

The only other place for deaf children was the Partial Hearing

Unit, but only 'successful' deaf children went there, or those with a lot more hearing than Sarah.

Sarah, it seemed, was too oral for the School for the Deaf, and too deaf for the Unit. Even so, the Unit, I now realized, was the place Sarah should be.

I went to see Sarah's teacher. While I waited in the classroom for her, I watched Sarah through the window with her little Indian friend Naima. They were standing facing one another deep in conversation. I saw them talking about Fiona's yellow dress and her hairstyle. They discussed their favourite colours, Naima's was red and Sarah's blue, then Sarah said she wanted to grow her hair, and to change the colour because she loved Naima's hair more than anyone else's. *All this without a single word being spoken.*

It was moving to watch them together, but what really made me gasp was the fluency of Sarah's sign language. Sarah, who needed practice of putting thoughts into words, was not speaking.

When Sarah had first started to use sign language to replace speech, I had shrugged my shoulders and said, 'What do you mean Sarah? I can't understand you when you sign. You'll have to speak to me.'

Sarah had accepted my limitations and after a while all signing at home ceased. In this way Sarah's double life began with 'home' pulling her in one direction, and 'school' pulling her in another. In the classroom she spoke to her friends as signing wasn't allowed. In the corridor, the playground, and on the bus, she signed and behaved in the same way as the other children. At home it was expected she behave in accordance with our ways, they were the only ways we knew, but it was like fighting a losing battle as her behaviour, which was never examplary, deteriorated.

I found Sarah's teacher to be in favour of her going to the Partial Hearing Unit, but when I spoke to the Head he said he didn't want to risk putting Sarah in a situation she might not be able to cope with; that she was happy where she was; and that she could not yet follow other *children's* speech.

He could not possibly have realized the anguish his decision would cause.

After a few weeks I went to see the Head again and he must have had time to reconsider his decision because he told me he would deal with the whole question after the summer holidays with a view to Sarah having a trial period in the Unit after Christmas.

I was both relieved and disappointed. Relieved because he had changed his mind, and disappointed because Christmas was so far away, and it was a struggle to keep Sarah ahead in her work all the time.

When the summer holidays were over I brought the subject up with the Head again, only to hear him say; 'Sarah's not emotionally ready for the Unit.'

I could argue on academic grounds for Sarah moving, I could argue for her speech now that she was understanding hearing children (well one or two of them anyway), but how could I argue with 'emotional readiness'? This inferred Sarah might not be happy in the Unit and the Head knew we would never put Sarah's academic progress before her happiness.

'You wouldn't want Sarah to fail because we've moved her too soon,' he had said. 'If she had to come back to this school she would feel she had failed.'

I couldn't get it out of my mind. The worry was with me all the time. Every single day mattered.

In November we heard about a new hearing-aid, a radio-telemetry aid.

It worked on the same principle as a policeman's walkie-talkie. There was the aid (or receiver) to be strapped to a child's chest, but, unlike an ordinary aid, it was radio-linked to a microphone which could be worn around a parent's neck. This meant that the parent (or teacher) could move around a room without the encumbrance of trailing wires, yet his voice be as clear to the child as if there were only a few centimetres between them.

The trouble with ordinary hearing-aids is that they begin to lose their effectiveness once a speaker moves out of their range: one moment the deaf person can hear a voice and the next not.

A trial was arranged for Joanne as it was thought Sarah's loss would be too severe to benefit, but when we arrived at the hospital she refused to wear the aid. Instead Sarah tried it on. It was bigger than her own aid and looked like something from outer space.

I put the microphone on, then stood behind Sarah. In front of her was a table on which stood several objects chosen for their sound content.

'GIVE ME THE DUCK,' I said loudly into the microphone.

Sarah hesitated then picked up the duck and handed it to me.

'Give me the STRING.'

Again, hesitation . . . then she passed me the string.

'Give me the cup.' I spoke in a normal sounding voice.

Sarah passed me the cup.

I might have conquered Everest. There was no doubt in my mind that Sarah would have the aid no matter what it cost. Like a blind person seeing shapes for the first time, Sarah would hear the outline of words more clearly than before.

We brought the aid home on a ten-day trial and Mick tested Joanne in the same way that Sarah had been tested by me in the hospital. First he used a normal-sounding voice and then he gradually reduced it to a whisper. A whisper.

Joanne had never responded so well before. I didn't have to ask Mick if he could buy the aid. He had seen the results for himself. He was with me.

I made appointments to see members of both the Education Authority and the Health Service the same week. Despite the proven superiority of the radio-telemetry aid over ones already provided for Sarah and Joanne on the National Health service, neither felt they could assist either in purchasing the aids, or in helping us to buy them.

We went to see the Bank Manager for a loan.

Joanne was a different child now. She was, we discovered, an essentially 'hearing' individual rather than a deaf one, and able to use lipreading to assist hearing, and not the other way round (as with Sarah). The difference in terms of usefulness between her ear-level aid and the radio-telemetry aid was almost as wide as that between her wearing her ear-level aid and not wearing an aid at all. Her speech would improve.*

But was it again too late for Sarah?

The possibilities which the aid brought were endless. Sarah could wear hers to school and be in contact with her teacher and receiving sound of a *constant* high quality. At home I could wear the microphone with Joanne, and when Sarah returned from school, I could change the frequency modulator on her aid so that either Mick or I could wear a microphone and be linked to them both . . .

It was during the trials for the aid that I saw Joanne's audiogram for the first time, and the shock stunned me for days. She didn't have a partial hearing loss as I had imagined. Nor was she partially deaf.

---

* Within six months Joanne's speech had improved to the extent that it was considered 'normal'. The radio-telemetry aid was also profoundly to affect her ability to cope in the ordinary school system.

Joanne had a severe hearing loss.

For the first twenty-two months of her life then, she would only have heard sound if it was close to her ear and loud. Even then she could hardly have known words. Not with that degree of loss.

Miss Ayling explained it to me:

'This is an audiogram of a normally hearing person. It shows where you begin to hear,' she pointed to the 'o' decibel level, 'and where, in the frequency range, speech occurs.' She pointed to the hertz.

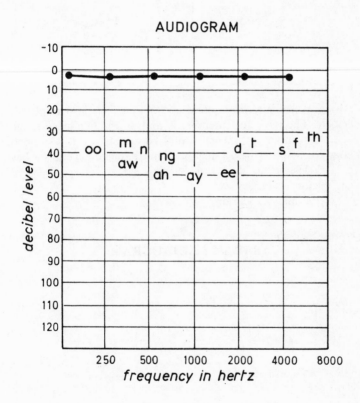

AUDIOGRAM

'A normally hearing person's threshold is 'o' decibels then, and conversation is found in the 30–60 decibel level range. There, you can see those letters on the audiogram. Now we'll look at Joanne's audiogram.'

JOANNE'S AUDIOGRAM

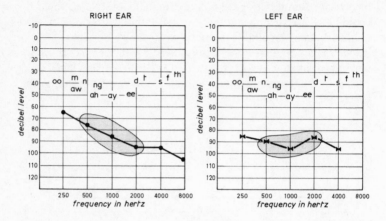

'Joanne begins to hear sound at "65" decibels instead of "0" decibels. The thing to remember is that, in the frequency range where the important speech sounds occur, between 500–2000 hertz,' Miss Ayling drew a ring round the frequency levels, 'she has an *average* loss of "85" decibels in her right ear, and an *average* loss of "90" decibels in her left ear.

'Now Sarah's audiogram.

SARAH'S AUDIOGRAM

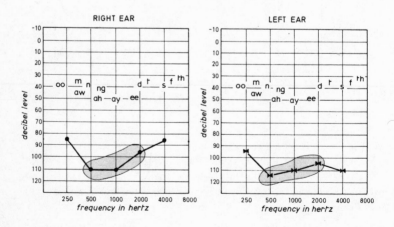

'Sarah begins to hear sound at "85" decibels, and again, where the important speech sounds occur, she has an *average* loss of "105" decibels in her right ear and a "110" decibel loss in her left ear.'

So how had Joanne ever passed a screening test? Let alone Sarah. Had the test sounds been too loud? They should have been at minimal levels of loudness. A sound-level meter would have ensured this.

Had the health visitors been adequately trained to carry out these tests? Had their own hearing been tested? It was interesting to note that the only person to state Joanne to be definitely deaf was the student who specialized in hearing impairment.

Had Joanne seen the movements of the health visitor behind her? She would have had good peripheral vision. Did she feel air on her neck as the rattle was shaken, respond to a waft of perfume, a movement by me, a sound in the room, or a reflection in the window? Had Joanne been able to sense the presence of a vibrating object where we as hearing people could not?

Had the test material contained high and low sounds separately? If not, Joanne may have responded to the low-tone content only.

Or had Joanne deduced, and this was the most likely explanation, that when all movement in front of her stopped, she was expected to turn? A trial period without sound would have eliminated this possibility.

And, in the test where instructions were given, had Joanne assumed an illusion of competence when it had in fact all been intelligent guesswork?

But the most significant indication of a hearing loss wasn't provided by a test at all. It was provided by a child development chart. This showed Joanne's language to be retarded. And why would her language development be retarded? Because she had a hearing loss.

18.   Concert and fire engines

Sarah was to have a 'speaking' role in the Christmas concert at
school and when we got to her classroom, Joanne, quite carried
away by the occasion, proceeded to tell all the children what the
other children were saying, whether they wanted to know or not.

'Tarah. Tarah. Fiona said for you to tie her ribbon.'

'Fiona. Fiona. Tarah said she will tie your ribbon.'

Joanne's role as interpreter for Sarah had begun the moment she
began to speak. If she was in the possession of information then she
immediately passed that information on to Sarah. A few months
ago, a teenage girl had spoken to Joanne on the beach and Joanne
straightaway told Sarah what she had said. The girl spoke to
Sarah. Joanne re-arranged the sentence so that Sarah would
understand.

'Are they both deaf?' the teenager asked curiously, and before I
could reply, Joanne piped up with, 'Tarah's deaf but I'm not.'

But for all that Joanne tried to include Sarah that day, Sarah was
on the outside. Quietly she watched from the fringe. And it
saddened me: her learning what it meant to be deaf.

At Sarah's school party the previous week, there had been a
woman like that – on the fringe. She was the deaf mother of a deaf
child in Sarah's class, and no one had been able to speak her
language: sign language.

It had taken a lot of courage for me to walk across the room to sit
beside her because I was afraid she might rebuff me.

'Hello.'

She nodded without smiling.

'Where's your little boy?' I asked, knowing exactly where he
was. I held my hand out at waist level.

But my bungling attempts at conversation, her own lack of
response made it seem as if I was patronizing her, and the more I
tried the worse it became. I struggled to make sense of her words. I
listened for their intonation and rhythm. And I watched her face

and body for clues. In those minutes my mind explored a thousand possibilities. Sarah and Joanne had to do that every day.

I was deeply frustrated by my inability to communicate with the woman. I had wanted her to tell me what it was like to be deaf. I wanted her to tell me so that I would know what it meant for Sarah to be deaf. Yet how many times in a day did she feel the way I felt now? She, who lived in a society which held all the cards, where even a trip to the shop was fraught with obstacles to overcome.

Joanne and I left Sarah's classroom to go to the school hall. There, the infant class were being led on to the stage as the lights dimmed. Sarah was dressed as a peasant girl with a red spotted headscarf. Her hair was back from her face and she had two patches of blusher on her cheeks, and pink lipstick smudged on her lips.

The mime of the Golden Goose began and I wondered at the industry and faith behind such a venture. Most of the children had little appreciation of the story, and indeed of a story itself. They saw the mime as many separate events and actions to be performed, so it was not surprising it came over to us disjointed and stilted.

As the children couldn't receive their cues from a script or the piano, they had to watch for a flashing light, a nod or a wink, and, failing that, there was always a prod to remind them from a teacher crouching behind the scenery.

A little boy came on to the stage with a huge grin. He was dressed as a woodcutter is supposed to be dressed, but his hobnail boots were at least three sizes too big for him. Still, his grin was bigger, making it even more difficult to think that this striking-looking child was actually deaf. It was touching now, with him a child, but it would be difficult for him to be a man. Much more difficult in some ways, I think, than for a deaf woman.

He raised his axe to begin chopping at the cardboard tree in the centre of the stage then turned to smile at the audience. I felt sure he didn't known why we were here. The teacher gave him a thumbs-up sign and dutifully he raised his axe again.

Someone flicked the light-switch off and on. He nodded and laid his axe down on the floor, carefully untied his spotted handkerchief and removed what he thought was a cardboard biscuit, at least that was what it had been in rehearsal. When he put it to his mouth and tasted its sugary coating an enormous smile crossed his face.

The rest of the performance was as disarmingly poignant with the children's lack of sophistication both compelling and

frightening. How many of these small unworldly beings would grow
to be big unworldly beings without this school to shelter and
protect them?

Sarah had rehearsed her part in the play over and over again and
the long awaited words came towards the end of the mime:

'I'm stuck.'

They remain to this day imprinted on my heart.

It was a much dwindled audience which stayed to watch the
senior school's Nativity play, and from the moment Mary and
Joseph entered, and Mary spoke, we were captured. The effort it
took for her to say her words seemed to come from every ounce of
her being, and we sat on the edge of our chairs, willing, willing,
them on.

The lights dimmed, the piano played the opening bars of *Silent
Night* and a few children, unsure of where to begin, started to sing.
Their voices rose and fell, then petered falteringly to a stop. From
out of the darkness came the sound of one parent's voice. Then
other parents joined in, their voices rising in simultaneous accord.
The children looked towards us, expressions of relief and gratitude on their faces, then they too joined in the singing. The sound
grew until the hall echoed with triumph as *Silent Night* was sung in a
way it would never be sung again. The children's voices were
tuneless and flat, their words recognizable only through the hymn,
but it was the most moving tribute ever.

Yes it was a special school – and they were special children.

'How can I talk about things which Sarah can't actually see?' I had
asked Miss Ayling.

This had been on my mind for ages now. I wanted to talk about
Mick at work, policemen, holidays, fun-fairs, airports . . . anything
which might interest her, because if she was interested she would
learn. The whole world was out there for the taking but for us it
might as well have been a world away.

'You could always take her to different places,' Miss Ayling had
suggested. And so we went to a fire station. It was a modern
brick building not far from the comprehensive school where
Mick taught and I asked the receptionist if I could speak to the
inspector.

Before long a tall, middle-aged man dressed in a uniform came
towards us. 'You wanted to see me?'

'Sarah and Joanne are deaf.' I blurted it out even before he had
had time to shake my hand. 'I'm trying to help them to talk but I

can't talk about things which they haven't seen for themselves, so I wondered if you would mind showing them a fire-engine and then I could take a photo of them beside it, and this will remind them of the engine when I talk about it afterwards at home.' I took a deep breath.

The inspector looked at me and Sarah and Joanne and said nothing. Then he turned and spoke into a microphone on the desk behind him but I couldn't hear what he was saying. Sarah and Joanne started doing handstands on the floor.

I was just about to explain myself further when a bell sounded throughout the building and several firemen appeared from a hole in the ceiling, to slide in rapid succession down a pole to the ground.

With the bell resounding in my ears, the inspector beckoned us to follow and we ran into a cloakroom to find the firemen donning protective clothing from a row of pegs lined with bright yellow helmets. Even before the helmets were on their heads, they were on the move again, and running through another door which led to an enormous glassed area almost the size of a football pitch.

One of the firemen ran to open a section of the folding doors, another started one of the three gleaming fire engines, two climbed on the back, and, after Sarah and Joanne had agreed to it, they whisked them into the cab. They waved as the engine drove off, its siren wailing.

In the silence which followed, the inspector and I stood side by side and watched the engine as it disappeared from sight. If only I could tell him how much this would mean to Sarah and Joanne in terms of the language they would gain – and how much it meant to me.

The firemen brought Sarah and Joanne back after they had hose-piped the fire engine and climbed all the ladders there were to climb, and the inspector escorted us around the rest of the building. We saw the games room, the dormitories, and the dining-room; and when the routine had been explained to me, I simplified it and repeated it for Sarah and Joanne. Finally, I took a photograph of everyone standing beside the fire engine.

In the past hour Sarah and Joanne hadn't understood a word of what had been said to them by anyone other than me, but they had been given more than words. They had seen a number of people go out of their way for them because they had cared enough to. And I had had my belief confirmed. People did want to help, and would go to any lengths to do so, provided they knew exactly what was required of them.*

It took me a while to understand the full meaning of the next step, and when I did it was a revelation. It wasn't only Sarah and Joanne who were discovering a previously unexplored world.

They now carried certain images of the fire station in their memories. What I was going to do was to ask them to carry those experiences forward in time as it were, and to talk about them as though they were present and before them. To do this they needed to be able to recall. I could help them to do this by saying, 'Do you *remember* when we went to the fire station?'

How could I explain 'remembering'? In hearing children abstract concepts develop over time. I would just have continually to repeat the word in the right context. It was amazing how one small phrase could act like a switch in the memory and from that we could recall a whole experience.

Obvious though it was, it had not occurred to me that if a deaf child did not form certain concepts, then his or her perception of the world must necessarily be different from that of a child who does form them. Moreover this limited perspective could quite feasibly stay with him or her until adulthood.

Sarah's development did not follow the same step-by-step stages as a hearing child's development so her thinking was different to a hearing child's thinking of the same age. Yet, because I was trying to treat Sarah normally, I did not fully appreciate this. I failed to see things from her point of view.

I failed to understand her.

---

* This visit was followed by one to a nursing home, a police station, a bakery . . .

19.   *Progress*

When Joanne went into the infant class after the Christmas holidays, she was at least a year ahead of the other children. She was also the youngest.

'Her comprehension is remarkable,' said her teacher. 'She's a fluent reader, her number work is excellent, and her written work is very good.'

If anything happened to Joanne's hearing now, she would have this grounding to support her.

On the morning of her first day at 'proper' school, I dressed her in a new, grey, pleated skirt and a pale-blue shirt. I knotted her new striped tie, plaited her thick brown hair, then strapped her cream-coloured hearing-aid over her royal-blue sweater. In her satchel was a hanky, an apple, a book for the journey to school, a brand-new pencil and rubber, the microphone which had been charged overnight in a battery-charger, one pair of black plimsolls, and a pair of navy gym knickers.

By the time she came home, the apple would be a discoloured core at the bottom of the bag, the hanky would be in its original clean condition, her plaits would be loose, and possibly one or two slides missing, her tie would be around her waist, and the buttons on her sweater would be undone. Gravy stains wouldn't fleck her school tie as with other small children but be congealed to her hearing-aid, causing normal tones to become gravy tones. She would come in singing, fling her arms round my neck and hold me tight – and not for one moment would she suspect that her sunny presence had been sorely missed.

Joanne did lose a lot of what was said in class even with her new hearing-aid, though there was still much in her favour. She was in a small class of eighteen pupils (initially for three days a week), she had our support and Miss Ayling's who went to the school once a week, and her very helpful teacher. As for Joanne, she loved her work, was attentive, and she applied herself enthusiastically to everything that went on in the school – sometimes too enthusiastically. When the class was told to get undressed for games, Joanne did – completely.

At no other time would Joanne's schooling be as difficult for her, and yet she gave no indication of this to us. Our thoughts were centred upon Sarah's more complex problems in her protected environment. Joanne had to make her own way, work out her own problems. She was the one who must adjust, not the school adjust to her.

At school Joanne met with incomparable kindness. They all wanted to understand, and went out of their way to do so, but they were the first to admit they were only learning too. It was Joanne who must pioneer a way.

If she didn't hear the children's conversation, she pretended to hear it. She laughed when the other children laughed, even though she didn't know why they were laughing. She pretended she didn't mind wearing a hearing-aid, when she minded terribly.

Because Joanne wanted to be the same as her friends, because being the same, in her eyes, meant being accepted.

Joanne never showed she minded these things because she had discovered the secret of deafness. Something in her told her that if she wanted to be the same as everyone else, then she had to act the same as everyone else. Joanne worked very hard at being the same. Very hard.

But with each hour she spent in an ordinary school, Joanne was becoming more like a hearing child. Not because her hearing was improving, but by being exposed to life. New situations quickly became old situations. Hard situations became easy ones. When a deaf child is isolated from such experiences he becomes 'deaf' in the truest sense of the word. And perhaps the truest sense of the word is 'isolated from life'.

If Joanne wanted to know what the children were saying, she had to use every ounce of concentration to listen. She had to learn to lipread every mouth: mouths that moved rapidly, mouths sideways on, mouths with lisps, and mouths that changed subject every second breath. She had to find out what she hadn't heard, and who best to discover it from.

The driving force behind this was Joanne's need to know. To be in a group and not know was a worse situation, I felt, than would be a term in solitary confinement.

Deafness though, whatever the attempts made to overcome it, has certain inherent limitations. So Joanne had to learn to rely on her wits. It wasn't her listening, lipreading, or academic ability, which would help her, so much as her wits.

Even so at some point each day, and maybe many times a day, deafness let Joanne down badly. These experiences shaped her. She was popular but she rarely pushed herself forward. In a group she was more vulnerable than any other child. To make a contribution Joanne had to be sure of herself, and there was one thing with deafness you could always be sure of, and that was you could never be sure.

Joanne had one special friend. Veronica, since the age of three, had run in circles to face Joanne and repeat conversations which she instinctively knew Joanne hadn't heard or understood. She changed the vocabulary, simplified the language, and she spoke purposefully clearly for Joanne to lipread.

Veronica also told her the day-to-day information without which Joanne would have stayed on the fringe of school life, the notices in assembly, the rhyme in the skipping game, the change in the lesson, or the hundred-and-one other things which fill a child's day. Veronica was thoughtful without thinking, generous without trying, kind without realizing it.

Veronica was as true a friend as any little girl could wish to have.

'Mummy.'

'Yes Joanne.'

'You can cough at school but you can't yawn.'

'I'll try and remember that Joanne.'

Sarah continued to go to the School for the Deaf; and she was reading.

It had been a long hard haul but Sarah recognized that the written word had a use, and it could work for her. The breakthrough came when she was five years old after I had made two large notices for Sarah and Joanne to pin on their bedroom doors.

Joanne read her notice. Even when she hadn't met certain words before she still attempted to read them by breaking them down into smaller units and saying them in different ways until they sounded right to her. How she deduced how words should sound may have been due to the auditory training unit. It was likely that those sound patterns, and not the sound patterns she heard through her first inadequate ear-level aid, were the model by which all incoming sounds were compared. And it was probable that those memory traces became the model for her speech.

'Thid is Carah . . .' Sarah began but she made no attempt to continue when she saw an unfamiliar word.

'This is Sarah's *bedroom*,' I read. '*Private. Keep out*. It's to hang on your bedroom door,' I explained.

In a blinding flash Sarah saw the potential of words. Words had power.

Words could keep Joanne out of her bedroom!

It was a lift in the uphill grind for Sarah as she tried to commit new words to memory, and I received more intense pleasure from hearing her read a single page than in Joanne reading a whole book.

And the reason for this was that the disability they shared could in no way be compared.

It is conceivable that, had Joanne received a diagnosis of her deafness in the early weeks of life, she could have followed the same developmental stages as a hearing baby, *and at the same time*.

Deafness was different for Sarah. It not only retarded her development, it actually *interfered* with the way she learned.

At birth Sarah had been (almost) at the same stage of development as any other baby but she grew away from her hearing. She developed to be 'deaf'. We were helping her to be someone who functions as a hearing person in the widest sense of the word. Not a child who is isolated from life: 'deaf' in the truest sense of the word.

20. The breakthrough

'Happy birthday Jo,' Mick murmured, as Joanne climbed over him, not caring where she put her feet, to snuggle between us in the warmth of the bed.

I pulled the curtains open. 'Happy birthday Joanne,' I said, kissing her. 'Put your hearing-aid on and. . . . Tell her will you Mick.' Joanne had looked away before I could finish.

'Put your hearing-aid on Joanne.' Mick motioned for her to do it.

Joanne pulled the hearing-aid out from amongst the presents she had brought with her from her room, and, kneeling up on the bed, put it on, tested it, and proceeded to feel her presents. She would never have opened them without Sarah.

'Jo. Go and tell Sarah to come in,' Mick said, and Joanne climbed over him to run to the door, her nightie billowing in her haste.

Sarah came straightaway, her manner expectant.

'Here's some presents for you too Sarah.' Mick pointed to some small packages by the bed. 'Say "Happy birthday" to Joanne,' he reminded her.

'Habby birthday Goanne.' Sarah distractedly put her arms round Joanne, straining to see over her shoulder to where Joanne's presents lay.

Jealousy was by far the most difficult emotion for Sarah to come to terms with and control. This morning she was to resolve it in a surprisingly mature manner.

We had been preparing her for this day for a while, encouraging her to think how she would feel if it was her birthday, and explaining that no matter what she felt inside, she must be glad for Joanne.

'That lovely Goanne,' she said, with each present Joanne opened. 'I glad you god it.' Her face was labouring with the effort of masking her true feelings.

'Good girl,' I encouraged, as the tension ballooned inside her.

I knew all children had jealous feelings but deafness somehow exaggerated this 'normal' behaviour to an 'abnormal' extent. Hearing children constantly modify or control their actions because of what they hear around them. Deaf children don't have the same opportunity to do this, simply because they are deaf. And Sarah's jealousy stemmed from her deafness: and Joanne.

Sarah was fifteen months old when Joanne was born and at first she was both tender and protective towards her. But then Joanne changed from the passive baby she was, to one who demanded, and worse, crawled. Each move she made filled Sarah with an intense anger as she ran to guard her possessions (all things) and her territory (the whole house).

My heart sank every time she pounced on Joanne, pulling her hair, scratching and biting. I tore them apart and wept to see the hurt Sarah had inflicted. I soon learned never to leave the two of them alone, for in these moments Sarah would strike with whatever was near at hand. Despite my attempts to distract her, and in the end smack her, *nothing* I could do had a lasting effect.

It seemed that I was always scolding Sarah and, because of this, I didn't immediately intervene when I saw Sarah dangle a golliwog temptingly above Joanne's face, daring her to touch it. Joanne who was lying on her back on the floor, kicked her legs excitedly as the toy swung slowly to and fro.

'Give Joanne the golliwog Sarah,' I said. 'You mustn't tease her.' But she ignored me and withdrew the golliwog from Joanne's reach. Joanne lay still, disappointed.

Sarah dangled the golliwog in front of Joanne's face again and when Joanne kicked her heels excitedly, she slowly removed it.

I watched with mounting misery as little by little Sarah encouraged Joanne into an excited frenzy and she leapt for the golliwog. That was the moment Sarah had planned. She tore into Joanne in an uncontrollable passion.

'Stop it. Stop it!' I dragged Sarah away and she brought with her the golliwog and a handful of hair. Joanne sobbed in my arms, blood trickling from scratches on her face, teeth marks on her skin.

Half an hour later Sarah climbed into Joanne's pram and they played happily together as if nothing had happened.

Four years had passed since then and Sarah's jealousy had still not been resolved.

After Joanne had opened her presents, and Sarah had opened her gifts too, Sarah disappeared from the room. The minutes went by and we could hear her rummaging through the drawers and cupboards in the other bedrooms. Then it went quiet and we saw Sarah standing at the door, her arms full. The light from the hall was shining down on her and a serene calm glowed in her face. I relaxed. Whatever it was that had happened out there had solved something for her.

'Tarah. Tarah. You can choose one of my presents,' Joanne called, opening her arms towards them. 'Anyone you like.' She was on the floor by our bed and the presents were spread in front of her. She had discarded the wrapping-papers though her cards were in a neat pile.

'No, I all right.' Sarah crossed the room and kneeling on the carpet, emptied the objects out of her arms. One by one she positioned them on the floor in exactly the same way Joanne had done with her presents.

There was a shoulder-bag, blue, similar to the one Joanne had received. Twelve felt-tip pens. She put them next to Joanne's twelve felt-tip pens. A red purse with a zip. Joanne's was green but it had a zip. A pencil-case with a lid. A pair of . . .

When Sarah had sorted her 'presents' to her satisfaction, she looked up at Joanne. 'We play now.'

So Sarah had come through the test with flying colours. She was in control.

Another piece of jigsaw in place.

Sarah wasn't functioning as a 'hearing' child at the School for the Deaf.

The school had begun to turn into a prison in my mind. Many things worried me. That she was with deaf children all day and not learning language to the extent she might have had she been with hearing children; that her thoughts were being denied the freedom they might have had she been in another situation; that she wasn't practising her speech to the extent she might . . .

There was something else as well. Sarah was losing her innocence. The children at her school were more (overtly) sexual than other children. It was natural that they had grown to be aware of the signals their bodies gave them, but it was hard for me to close my eyes to this.

'Why don't you ring the Education Offices to find out why Sarah can't go to the Unit?' a friend suggested.

I had never thought of going behind the Head of the school's back, but I was desperate now and picked up the phone before I had time to think.

Sleep eluded me that night. When I had told Mick what I had done, he said, 'How do you *know* the Unit is the right place for Sarah?'

'I don't *know*. Nobody does until she goes there. I'm as sure as I can be though.'

'We don't want anything to reflect upon Sarah,' he replied.

I went to see the Special Education Adviser the next morning. 'Why do you want Sarah to go to the Unit?' he asked.

'I think she would benefit from going there. Sarah needs to be with hearing children.'

I knew from the start it was a hopeless task to make this man understand. My case was based upon feelings, and he comprehended only facts.

'Sarah understands about God and heaven,' I told him.

If I had said Sarah had reached a stage of conceptual development which no other child in her class had reached, he might have realized what I was trying to say. I didn't use words like that though.

The Adviser's manner was professional, diplomatic, but, as far as deafness was concerned, we weren't on the same wavelength.

When I stood up to leave he said, 'Of course I can't make any comment until I have spoken to the Headmaster.'

A few hours later: 'I have spoken to the Head of Service for the Hearing Impaired in this county,' the voice on the other end of the phone said formally. 'And his view is that Sarah is in the correct educational setting for her hearing loss.'

I managed to see the Head of Sarah's school again, but still my way seemed blocked. 'Please tell me once and for all why Sarah can't go to the Unit?' I asked him finally. 'I need to know so I can take this further.'

'Further. What do you mean?'

'I need to know because unless I do, I can't help.'

'Well,' he said. 'Sarah can't go because the Authority won't provide an assistant teacher in the Unit. The Headmistress of the infant school where the Unit is based will not have another child until they do.'

It was as if a brick wall had been knocked down and the sun allowed to shine in.

'Then I can help.'

'What do you mean?'

'If they need a teacher I'll offer my services.'

There was a momentary hush in which the Head's expression softened. '. . . It would have to be on a voluntary basis.'

'Nothing matters as long as Sarah can go to the Unit.'

'Leave it with me Mrs Robinson,' he was smiling broadly now. 'I'll put your proposal to the Authorities.'

Sarah started at the Partial Hearing Unit after the Easter holidays – and I began a day later.

21. *Who holds the key?*

Sarah's new school was surrounded by row upon row of terraced houses. As we entered the building, a huge swell of children came down the wide corridor. Then the door to the Partial Hearing Unit swung behind us and Sarah and I were left curiously insulated from the hustle and bustle outside.

The Unit was a bright, modern-looking classroom which was in sharp contrast to the rest of the school. The floor was carpeted, the walls thickly tiled, the windows double-glazed. Strip-lighting shone down on eight small children sitting at five grey tables, and along one wall was a frieze of three pigs 'huffing and puffing'.

The teacher raised her eyes from a child she was helping, then came forward to meet us. She was tall and slim, with brown hair, and she had an air of confidence about her.

When I left Sarah with her, and walked to the car, I thought of Sarah sitting down to dinner with four hundred children and not one of them a face she would know. I would have given anything to have made this easier for her.

'The children will miss Sarah,' they had said at the School for the Deaf, 'especially the boys. Sarah was great fun for the boys. But we'll all miss Sarah.'

Sarah would miss Mark, Fiona, Paul, Naima, and the other children too.

The following day I joined Hazel (the teacher) in the Unit. There the children's ages ranged from four to seven and they all integrated to some extent into an equivalent-aged class in the main school. At this level integration was for social rather than academic reaons, so the children joined the main school classes for subjects like library, games, painting or dancing, while the youngest amongst them ran along the corridor to the nursery.

The overall aim of the Unit was to bring the children to an academic standard level with the hearing children in the main school. Then, at the age of seven, they moved to the Unit at the

Junior School where integration was stepped up for them with the intention of achieving full academic and social integration by the age of eleven. They progressed from there to their local Comprehensive, or to a Comprehensive with a Unit, or to a school away from home.

In the Unit the children followed individual schemes of work set by Hazel yet within the framework of the main school curriculum. This could in effect mean that, when the children did number work for instance, there were eight different topics being worked on. When the children were grouped for their work, they were often grouped by age or friendship rather than ability, because no two children's ability was ever the same, and though this is true for all children, rarely is it to a similar extent.

Sarah worked quietly throughout the morning but every time Hazel's back was turned, her eyes pleaded with me to go to her. When this didn't work, she raised her hand in the air, but I stayed on the other side of the classroom to let Hazel see to her. As I worked, I could feel Sarah's eyes drilling into my back. Every sense within me cried out to go and comfort her.

At twelve o'clock, I went into the hall where Sarah was having her dinner to the tremendous sound of raised voices and dishes clattering. Sarah was flanked on either side by children from her 'hearing' class. She was wearing the same school shirt and tie she usually wore, yet there was something different about her. When she saw me, she smiled – and the weight of School for the Deaf fell from my shoulders.

It wasn't that Sarah had become less deaf all of a sudden, or that her deafness was denied. It had little to do with deafness at all. It had to do with the other children's *behaviour*. In a hearing-child's terms, Sarah was still emotionally immature, socially naïve, intellectually retarded, and with a narrow perspective on life. She barely knew the difference between right and wrong; she couldn't hold a conversation of any length or depth; she wasn't understood by most people, was often insensitive and selfish, and much more besides.

In this school deafness no longer overrode her personality as it had in the deaf school. Nor did it segregate her. Deafness wasn't the whole of her, but a very secondary thing.

These children could give Sarah something no deaf child could: it was 'ordinariness'.

I approached the table to a chorus of, 'Sarah's dropped her peas. Sarah's dropped her peas.'

'Don like peas,' she said, blushing a deep pink.

I crouched, and there, under Sarah's chair, were her peas, not scattered as one would expect, but in a neat pile.

After dinner Hazel said to me. 'We should have had Sarah much earlier.'

I nodded.

Sarah wasn't anywhere near the bottom of her age group in the Unit, and she was doing the same sort of work as hearing children of her age. By now I had discovered that a few of the children weren't partially hearing at all, but much more severely impaired. Some had even got more of a hearing loss and less language than many of the children in Sarah's class at the School for the Deaf. If these children can manage, I thought to myself, then so could at least three-quarters of those children too. I wonder if their parents realize this.

I couldn't understand the thinking behind it. Perhaps the mere existence of the School for the Deaf was considered enough justification for sending a child there, and naturally the school would resist attempts to reduce its numbers because this would, in the end, threaten its existence. Yet for the majority of deaf children, there were more benefits to be gained from a Unit placement than there were to be gained in a School for the Deaf.

Each morning the children would put on the radio-telemetry aids which had been donated to the Unit. When they were ready, Hazel plugged similar frequency modulators into the aids so that she was linked to all the children and, amid cries of 'My hein-aid not working,' and 'Mine broked,' the day began.

Sarah was very composed for the first few days, but when the tears came she clung to me in the same way she had at the nursery school. Time and time again I took her back to her seat as she sobbed; 'Home Bummy, home.' Before long though she had started copying the other children and putting her hand in the air when she wanted me. She still called me 'Bummy' but always with the added clarification for the other children's sake, '*My* Bummy.' From this she moved on to 'Miss Bobbins' or 'Kathy' depending on her mood.

I became fond of the children. It would have been hard not to when working with them at such close quarters, though communication difficulties were an ever-present barrier to getting to know them well. If I had a favourite I suppose it was Anne. She was typical of a very deaf child, if there ever was such a thing as 'typical'. Her changes of mood were rapid and unpredictable and she was infuriatingly difficult to 'reach'. She couldn't concentrate for any length of time; she had a roving restless energy; she lacked perseverance (with her schoolwork at least); and she had difficulty recalling words. Less typically, she wasn't unduly self-centred, ungrateful or thoughtless (or this didn't show at school), although she was stubborn and determined when it came to wanting her own way. If she was scolded she broke her heart, but only for a moment; the most important thing to her was that the children were her friends, and she found work an intolerable hardship. Beneath her cheeky smile and peals of trilling laughter, I could sense that Anne was a deeply troubled little girl.

Another child, Steven, was seven, with unruly blond hair and a disarmingly friendly grin. He was the most oral child in the Unit and he had a moderate hearing loss. His speech was good and he integrated with few problems. The Unit gave him just the support he needed because his poor reading skills caused his other work to suffer. Outside school, Steven used sign language with his deaf friends: he was the only child I knew who appeared to move with ease between both deaf and hearing worlds.

It was an ease which Sarah did not find when she integrated into the main school. To her, security was being surrounded by people who deferred to her hearing loss by facing her. In the 'hearing' class there were no simple means for her to learn rules and procedures when words were inconsequential movements on a teacher's lips. Sometimes I wondered what it was like for Sarah to walk through an immense hall with her microphone in her hand and to enter a classroom where the children's chatter was but an echo in her ear.

A good working relationship developed between Hazel and me, and when the Authority decided to make the position I was filling a permanent one, she encouraged me to apply.

The interview took place towards the end of the term and the only other person on the short list was a newly qualified teacher of the deaf from outside the area.

Half an hour later she was offered the post.

'You'll get over it,' Mick said. 'I'll take you out tonight to compensate.'

His words reminded me of something I had heard the Head-mistress of the school say to the Adviser after the interview was over. 'We all have our disappointments in life,' she had said. 'Mrs Robinson will just have to take the same knocks as everyone else.'

Sarah Robinson. Report. Age 6 years 2 months

Sarah has settled down well in the Unit, but is still very unhappy in the other class.

Number . . . Sarah can add and subtract, and knows the composition of numbers up to ten. She can tell the time on the hour, half an hour, and has just started doing the quarter hour. She knows the coins, and can add and subtract in simple 'shopping' situations. She has worked through the language of pre-measurement relations, and has measured feet and span. She has done some practical weighing.

Reading . . . Sarah has read the early 'Gay Way' books well. She has experienced some difficulty with the next stage of the reading scheme and needs a lot of supplementary material at her present level. She has been reading 'Breakthrough' books.

Written work . . . Sarah can be neat and she has a good written style. She can copy, and can work from simple cards involving finding the right word to put in a sentence etc.

Word building . . . is progressing nicely.

22.   *A furry friend*

'I can hear better.'

This advance, the most basic in the development of Sarah's hearing, had come about because I had had an ear mould made by the firm which supplied the radio-telemetry aids, instead of having one made through the National Health Service. Now I was able to turn the volume on her aid from its normal setting on '3' to its maximum setting on '9' – without it whistling!

I thought of the years when her hearing hadn't been fully utilized and I wanted to weep. Weep because of the sheer futility of it, and because it mattered. It mattered while her hearing was being trained. It mattered for her speech. Sarah had been wearing a hearing-aid worth hundreds and hundreds of pounds, and because of one worthless bit of plastic it hadn't even begun to touch her true hearing.

We had an ear mould made for Joanne and the improvement in her response to sound was even more dramatic.

This advance was followed by another. I had often wondered at the wisdom of stimulating Sarah's right ear only. There was a fear that prolonged amplification could damage remaining hearing though there was no proof this actually happened.

We bought another lead and had another ear mould made.*

The veil was finally drawn and my voice reached Sarah with a flow which can only ever be achieved through hearing. Every moment spent in training her hearing had paid off, for, while her actual hearing loss remained the same, her ability to pick up and interpret sound had improved. In future with practice of listening, with speech and language, with living, it would in this sense, get better and better.

---

* What was true for Sarah was true for Joanne as well.

Sarah wanted to share her seventh birthday. She invited all the neighbours, young and old alike. When she started inviting people in the shops too, we had to put a stop to her activities.

The children began arriving for the party and Sarah, in a blue corduroy dress and lace collar, welcomed them at the door with, 'I glad you come'. She thanked each child for their present, taking care not to make any one of them feel their gift was any less special to her, introduced the children to each other, and throughout the afternoon checked that everyone felt included. At the table she made sure they all had a place, re-arranged the chairs so everyone could sit where they wanted to sit, said. 'Have some more lemonade Christopher. Are you all right Claire' and 'I like your pretty dress Andrea'.

I stepped back to watch this self-possessed young lady in action, tingling with pride. She was much more the considerate, well-mannered and warm hostess than I could ever have hoped for and, though she was almost toothless at the time, she was charmingly so.

This birthday seemed to mean a coming of age to Sarah as she was for ever professing to be 'growed up' after that.

'I wan to go to the shop by mydelf,' she declared and, pulling on her anorak, made for the door.

'Hang on Sarah. Would you buy me a jar of coffee please?'

I hadn't been looking forward to this moment but in trying to steer Sarah and Joanne towards independence, we guarded against danger by preparing them for it.

'Don't forget to wait at the zebra crossing until a car actually stops before you cross,' I reminded her.

I knew Sarah would be careful on the crossing because last year I had smacked her leg for stepping off the pavement without looking to see if there was a car coming, and that was a lesson she would never forget. She had been mortified to be smacked in front of other people.

'What if the lady underdand me?'

Sarah must have suddenly realized Joanne would not be there to interpret for her as she usually was.

'The lady will understand you if you speak clearly. Say, "Could I have a jar of coffee please?" and then wait. If the lady doesn't move to get the coffee, say it again and point to the shelf. If she *still* doesn't understand, give her this note.' I quickly wrote a note and wrapped it round the money.

Sarah took the money with the note wrapped round it and ran

off. I thought it incredible that she was still prepared to go to the shop even when there was a real possibility of her not being understood. More times than I could count Sarah met situations which should have stripped her of all confidence, yet somehow her steely determination always pulled her through.

Sarah returned within a short while proudly bearing, not a jar of coffee, but a bar of toffee!

My grandfather died. 'He's gone to heaven,' I explained to Sarah and Joanne.

'How will he get there if he is buried?'

'Joanne, it's his *soul* which goes to heaven, not his body.'

Joanne accepted Grandpa's death more readily than Sarah because she believed he would be happier in heaven with Grandma than on earth without her. Sarah saw his death as a deprivation from Grandpa's point of view, from his dog's point of view, and a deep personal blow to her.

'What does a toul look like?' Joanne put her elbows on the table and her head in her hands.

'A soul isn't like a heart, something you can see. It's our being. It's us, what we are. Do you know what I mean?' I asked, and only Joanne nodded.

'What doul look like?'

'Sarah. Your soul is you. It's your goodness. What's inside you. . . . Grandpa had four children. What do you think they will be feeling now?' I wanted Sarah and Joanne to put themselves in their positions. To consider their feelings.

'The dog will be lonely.' Sarah said, showing where her sympathies lay.

'Perhaps you would like to draw a card so they will know you are thinking of them,' I suggested.

In time four cards lay on the table. Joanne had drawn Father Christmas on one of hers, and inside it she had written:

Dear Auntie,
I know that you are sad that Grandpa had died, but I am making you happy with this card.

On the front of Sarah's card was a crucifix with a wing on either side depicting Grandpa's upward flight, and on the inside she had drawn Grandpa. He had two very long legs, a smaller body and, on his considerably smaller head, perched his very favourite straw hat. Out of the corner of Grandpa's mouth was a filter-tipped cigarette, and the sun was shining in heaven. A large bubble emanated from his head and inside this was his dog. Evidently Grandpa's heavenly thoughts were with his dog, and, in Sarah's eyes, this was exactly how it should be.

Nothing more was mentioned about Grandpa until bed-time when Sarah burst into tears because, 'Gamma Bobbinson was getting old and had no Daddy,' and Grandpa Wingfield had died, and anyway his dog was going blind and Daddy was old enough to have a heart attack, and she didn't want him to have a heart attack 'cause it would 'broked her heart into little pieces'.

To distract her from this mournful flow I passed her a toy dog and a large bar of soap and motioned for her to 'wash' him. For a moment Sarah buried her head in his fur, sobbing, but soon she was so wrapt up in caring for him that she forgot about her tears, and she forgot about me.

She hugged him round the neck, and, making soothing sounds, she tucked him into bed. Next, she fetched a mirror and a bedside light, and with one hand on her hip she said to herself. 'What for his cupboard . . . I know,' and she ran from the room only to return a minute later with a shoe-box in her hand to use for his cupboard. Before long she had made a 'house' for her dog with everything in it she thought a dog might require.

These were magical moments when a lost childhood was re-trieved. To Sarah the dog was her feeling furry friend.

It was the first time I had seen her engrossed in imaginary play and the first time I had heard her 'think' out loud. She was seven years old.

Another piece of jigsaw in place.

Once upon a time I hadn't been able to see how Sarah would ever ask a question, now she was not only asking questions but working ideas out logically, taking them from one context to use in another.

One morning Sarah had greeted Grandma at the door by putting her hand on Grandma's chest to check that her heart was still beating. 'Gamma,' she said, 'I hope you don feel too old for your age. Don forget to take your medicine.'

Grandma, who was almost eighty, was overwhelmed by this. 'She really cares for me,' she said.

I think it was this, Sarah caring, which gave me an inner glow with which nothing else could compare.

I stayed stroking her forehead and humming next to her ear.

Every now and then she would move my hand to another position on her forehead and pat it to let me know she appreciated me being there.

She fell asleep clutching her dog. She had someone of her own to love, someone of her own to cuddle – and he was real, really real.

In general we now helped Sarah less than we had ever done. We could have given more but for Sarah's sake, if not our own, it was time to relax a little. She was getting through a lot of work during the day and this was cemented in her homework at night. It was this ten or fifteen minutes, adding up over the years to many hours' work over and above that which a hearing child is expected to do, which helped to lessen the gap between Sarah and hearing children of the same age. We encouraged this homework but we viewed it as Sarah's responsibility and not ours. It was an attitude which would in the end pay dividends.

Language was still the very best thing we could help Sarah with. Language held the key to her personality; to her emotional, social, intellectual, and indirectly, her physical self. Less importantly, it was upon Sarah's language that her school progress would depend.

Most of our attempts to explain anything were met with resistance so we had continually to think of new ways of presenting information to her. Sarah's single-minded, determined and independent spirit would be her strength in life: the day had yet to come though when it would work *for* her and not *against* her.

Every evening Sarah would lie on her bed reading cartoon books or easy readers – the easier the better – out loud to herself. At first I had puzzled about this because she didn't wear a hearing-aid in bed, then I realized she was 'hearing' herself reading through the vibrations in her throat and the movements of her mouth.

Reading aloud was a normal stage of development, what wasn't normal was Sarah's age when it occurred. But then almost every aspect of her development depended on the depth of concentration given to it at any particular time.

We tried to help Sarah in number-work: we played with money, but this led to arguments. Then one night we realized that deep down we should have hope, when Mick slipped his hand under her pillow and brought out a note she had left beside her tooth for the fairies.

It was short and to the point: '99p please.'

This was the time when the suffocating shell of deafness cracked and, as a butterfly would emerge from a chrysalis, Sarah escaped: free.

She called me a 'pest', wrapped Mick round her little finger, and nicknamed Joanne 'Jody'.

When, at the age of seven years and three months, she came to the end of her days in the Infant Unit, she had succeeded in doing something we had never dreamed she could. Sarah finished with her schoolwork on a par with the children in her 'hearing' class. It was a credit to Hazel, an accomplished teacher, even more it was credit to Sarah.

There was still a long way to go. Sarah couldn't find the right words to say what she wanted to say, nor put them in the right order to know what she wanted to know.

Sarah Robinson. Report. Age 7 years 3 months

Sarah has been in the Unit for just over a year. In that time she has absorbed a tremendous amount of material and fully justified everyone's confidence in her. She has shown herself perfectly capable of integration for social activities and could now benefit from some academic integration as she is on a par with her peers in number work, and her reading is good. Her 'news' has blossomed from nothing this year and she is beginning to show some aptitude for imaginative writing. She is still a little insecure however, and needs to be reassured periodically that she can manage. Given a sympathetic teacher in the Juniors, she should do well.

23.   *A new beginning*

'Why you have a heein-aid to hear with Mummy?' Sarah asked. Before I could reply she had tugged at the straps of her hearing-aid and deposited it on the table. 'I not wearin my heein-aid more,' she informed me.

'Why haven't I got a hearing-aid?' I repeated Sarah's words for Joanne and to give myself time to think. Joanne knew I didn't wear a hearing-aid because I could hear, and she knew Sarah wore one because she was *deaf*.

I realized it was better for Sarah and Joanne to become accustomed to hearing the word 'deaf' in an atmosphere of love, rather than to hear it from a child who might use it less kindly. But the word had been like a spectre. It was as if by using it I might transfer society's image of deafness upon them. In the end I got round the problem by injecting it with humour. Joanne picked it up and stopped me being afraid.

'Tarah,' she said, 'do you mind not shouting? You'll deafen me,' and she burst into peals of delicious laughter.

But now Mandy, Michelle, Sarah and Joanne waited for my answer. The hearing-aid was whistling on the table.

I went over to it and switched it off, pleased that Mandy and Michelle were here. Picking up the aid I said, 'Would you like me to wear it instead?'

Sarah nodded.

Holding the aid against my chest I fitted the ear mould into my ear, then, switching it on I visibly flinched before removing it again. 'Sarah it's too loud for me that's why I don't wear an aid. I don't need one. It's good for you because it helps you to hear.'

Mandy and Michelle were listening to every word, and though I didn't say their names, they knew they were included. I had never discussed Sarah and Joanne's deafness with them because over the years they had developed the same attitude as me towards it, though this is not to underestimate their own kind natures, or the influence of their own parents. It was because of them, I believe, that Sarah's teacher at the School for the Deaf could say that Sarah had the most normal behaviour in the class. The value of Mandy's and Michelle's friendship to Sarah was inestimable.

'God gave us all gifts for us to use,' I said. 'You can't hear very well, but you're kind Sarah, and Joanne, you're thoughtful. What else?' My words were contrived but they were the best I could do.

'I can run the fattest in the class,' Joanne replied, and ran on the spot to prove it.

'I beated all the boys in the Unit,' Sarah said, her face beaming.

'You beat all the boys in the Unit did you? There are so many things you can do. You can swim, dance, draw beautiful pictures.'

'You draw beautiful pictures Michelle.' Joanne smiled up at her. 'What wrong with you? . . . I wish you could be deaf Michelle,' she said quietly.

'Why Jo?' Michelle asked.

'Then we could all be deaf together.'

They had begun moving towards the door when I heard Sarah say: 'Michelle do you like me to be deaf?'

Michelle looked at me, a plea for help on her face. I whispered to her.

'Sarah, I like you just the way you are,' Michelle answered.

Sarah smiled up at her and took her hand. As they went outside to play Sarah's hearing-aid was once more firmly in place on her chest.

After the summer holidays Joanne started a new school. Sister and her staff had set her firmly on the road, now it was time she move down it.

She looked gorgeous in her new royal-blue sweater and matching tie. She was suntanned and her hair was spiked with gold. She had long athletic legs, and ever since her sixth birthday, three days ago, she had stopped sucking her thumb, wearing her cardigan inside out and leaving her shoes undone, though she had yet to learn what a comb was, and that Enid Blyton didn't belong in the loo.

At eight-forty-five we sauntered hand in hand through the village, past the shops and the newsagents where Sarah had bought her sweets all that time ago, past the church and into St Agnes's School.

It was a modern building with a large playground in front and a field behind where the children played in summer. It was spacious, open, and like a breath of fresh air to me.

On entering the school, Joanne took the teacher's proffered hand and, without a backward glance, went down the corridor.

This wasn't the first time I had had cause to admire Joanne. She knew the limitations her hearing imposed, and was wary of situations where it would let her down, causing embarrassment not only to her, but to others as well. She knew because it had happened many times before.

She would be aware that the staff and the children weren't always used to speaking clearly. She would be aware of her aid and what the children were thinking as the classroom door opened to thirty nameless faces. It was because she was aware, and yet still faced the test with composure, that she was courageous.

I knew she would smile at the children who had yet to learn how to speak to her, and try not to hide the hearing-aid on her chest, and the only indication of how she was feeling would be the pretty pink flush that came readily to her cheeks.

I thought of Miss Ayling. She would not, in a working capacity anyway, see either Sarah and Joanne again. But she knew the contribution she had made to Sarah's and Joanne's lives. She also knew there was a special place for her in my heart.

I thought of the time when the Headmaster had said when Joanne was only three, 'I hope one day Sarah and Joanne will come to us here at St Agnes's.'

And today Joanne had started St Agnes's School.

It was a new beginning.

The class teacher's report

The children readily accepted Joanne. After initial curiosity, to which she was most patient, Joanne was just another child in the class. She made friends easily and with one in particular, Zoë. I don't think Joanne was made to feel different from other children.

When reading together the group would sit in a circle and pass the microphone from one to another as they spoke. There was no fuss or silliness.

At first I stood near Joanne for class teaching but, after I found the range of the microphone, it was easier for me. There was no problem on a one-to-one basis.

When Joanne did not respond, one of the children would

touch her on the shoulder, and they did this without any direction from me. Zoë was good. She would take Joanne's arm and lead her, or point, to anything she had missed.

Joanne worked well. The content was good though untidy. She loved to read and her comprehension showed in her work. We did have a few problems with word building, but nothing which couldn't be overcome with practice.

24. *A continuing nightmare*

I came home in a daze. Sarah had come ninth out of twenty-nine in her first year at Junior School. I had neither expected nor deserved such rewards. Sarah, it seemed, was not only competing with hearing children, she was winning.

It was a rosy picture but one that did not tell the whole truth. Sarah was receiving a great deal of individual attention suited to her needs, both in the Unit and at home. Exams didn't reflect her progress beyond the narrow confines of the curriculum. And no exam result could ever give me as much satisfaction as to hear Sarah reason in spoken language. 'Mummy,' she said. 'If Ian went to Ameica to be peeceman, I could be a peecewoman and we could get married.'

It is said that when blind people become sighted it is the minutiae of detail which means everything to them. In a way it was like that for me. At the age of seven and a half Sarah's grammar wasn't always perfect but her choice of words was original:

'Where the Holy man?' (The Priest).

'Thank you for the toy rabbit, thinks me of Snowy.' (Reminds me.)

There was her first sarcastic comment: 'You're creasing my bag. Well done.'

and all those lovely expressions: 'It up to you.' 'What a bore.' 'Oh well.' 'If I . . .'

The context was usually right but: 'Was she over the mood?' (The moon). 'Susan's got lentils in her eyes.' (Lens). 'Floody bell!'

After Mick had explained about Good Friday she asked: 'Was that before Elvis was born?'

Sometimes she became confused between what she saw and other people heard: 'Did you hear the lightning Mummy?'

It had taken five long years for Sarah to have thoughts and to speak them fluently. Now Sarah's work reflected her command of language, and her command of language was improved by her work. Language was an aid to her hearing, and her hearing was an aid to her language.

I had often felt a sense of achievement with Sarah, but it was only now I knew what I had achieved. To raise a child to a level of consciousness ready to go forward into the world as a rational human being was surely the most fulfilling of all my given tasks.

In the eyes of the world, though, talking had little value. Our friends' children talked. The children in the Unit talked. The children in the main school talked. At the Junior School there was nothing special about that. Because of this Sarah was seen not so much by what she *had* achieved but by what she *had not* achieved.

Often learning was made unduly difficult for her. 'I don't think she hears me,' said her teacher in the 'hearing' class, while others complained they had problems understanding her, on top of which they had to repeat things for her. They spoke as if it was Sarah's *fault* they couldn't understand her, as if they blamed her for the extra effort they had to make. Others gave the impression they were doing her a favour, having a deaf child in their class. They quite failed to see that Sarah had as much right to be in their class as any other child. She was their responsibility too.

So Sarah went on with her drawing, or copying from the blackboard, then gratefully returned to the Unit. But for the fact that the other children in the Unit had to integrate also, her trips must have seemed almost like a punishment for being deaf.

At home, if pressed, her comments were always similar: 'I don't understand a single word of Mrs. . . . She keep moving around too quickly. I ask her what she says but she said I should have been consecratin.'

'Concentrating.'

'Yes, consecratin.'

It was only now that we began to pay positive attention to Sarah's schoolwork. At home we had time for all the repetitive chores: the spellings, times tables or counting, chores for which there was no other solution but to learn and forget, and learn all over again.

There was much more now which Mick and I could be interested in, and much as a family we could explore. Geography was a holiday where maps were drawn and photographs taken. History was a trip to London and the crown jewels. Science had begun long before with a bowl of water and a sieve. One visit, one new experience were the foundations of learning whose branches would extend for years.

We tried to give mathematics meaning by carrying Sarah's schoolwork into everyday life. We weighed cake ingredients, measured curtains, counted sweet money, and we dotted our conversations with mathematical concepts: difference, divide, calculate and total.

We made stories up to help her creative writing, played games with commas and capitals, and we relayed current events. There was still a world out there needing to be interpreted, to give meaning to schoolwork and meaning to life.

A seven-year-old, however, has much more important things to think about than work. Sarah joined a gym class, the Brownies tried a ballroom dancing class. . . .

Sarah and Joanne attended the dancing classes for a term, then a competition was held between the various schools in the area. The event took place in a nightclub and a hundred children, dressed in black patent shoes and glittering ball dresses with layers of petticoats, practised their dance steps on the wooden floor. Sarah and Joanne looked sweet and natural beside them in their plain pink and white dresses.

The competition started. With the microphone already next to the record-player, Sarah and Joanne stepped on to the dance floor to join the children there.

When the music began to play, Sarah missed the opening bars of the Cha Cha, and the Head of the school quickly crossed the floor to dance the first steps with her. Holding the hems of their dresses, and with their heads held high, Sarah and Joanne danced first the Cha Cha, then the waltz. In the space of seconds Joanne was transformed into a child light on her feet and unbelievably graceful, while I simply could not take my eyes from Sarah.

They heard the music as a gross sound, rather like hearing humming instead of singing. The vibrations from the music were absorbed into their bodies giving them a finer sense of rhythm than many people, not necessarily because they felt it more, but because they relied on it more.

When the dancing had finished, and the applause was over, a teacher from another school came over to say, 'They're naturals,' and later, as we turned to leave, the Head of the school said quietly: 'Thank you for bringing them.'

It was the greatest compliment I could have been given.

We arrived home, Sarah with two medals, Joanne with a cup

and a medal. Joanne put hers on the side and said, 'I don't want to go again.'

These activities, dancing, Brownies, or tap dancing, none of which endured, were less time-consuming than the hours spent playing with Mandy and Michelle and the other children who lived nearby, reading, watching television, or swimming. There was a lot in fact for a seven-year-old to do.

But Sarah still lacked a certain dimension to her personality. She was an independent spirit, a child without purpose or unity. Joanne had a richness and depth which Sarah did not possess. I believed Joanne had found this at St Agnes's school. There she was inextricably linked to every teacher and child. There was one thread, a common bond. I wanted this for Sarah and for her to make friends of her own age in her own neighbourhood. I couldn't see any reason why she couldn't integrate into St Agnes's in the same way she was doing in the Junior School, even if it was only for half a day a week at the start (I was willing to transport her). Besides, the prospect of her attending St Agnes's in the future could be assessed. However, despite having the support of the Headmaster of St Agnes's, my request was turned down.

All would have stayed as it was had not events conspired to make us continually request that Sarah had a trial period at St Agnes's School.

I felt that if Sarah could be satisfactorily supported, she would receive far greater advantage on a social and emotional level *both now and for the rest of her life*, from attending her local school rather than a Unit eighteen miles away, though she would not benefit academically to the extent she would in the Unit.

By this time a new Head of Service for the Hearing Impaired had come to the area, and he brought with him a whole new philosophy to the education of the deaf.

It was called *Total Communication*.

This method of communication had begun some years earlier in the United States and had gained in popularity despite intense opposition from the Oralists who condemned it as 'signing by another name.' Where before it was Oralism versus Signing – now it was Oralism versus Total Communication.

Total Communication was what it inferred – a total way of communicating. To this end it used sign language, finger-spelling, lipreading, listening and speaking. Total Communicationalists believed a child must learn language and be able to communicate – no different to the Oralists' way of thinking – except that, to achieve this, they used whatever means of communication they had available to them. Many figures were produced in support of this argument, figures which showed that under the Oralist system the vast majority of deaf school-leavers had unintelligible speech, that their average reading age was eight years, that deaf children were no better lipreaders than hearing children. . . .

Total Communication seemed to have the answer to everything that was wrong with the education of the deaf.

But there were implications.*

At the very moment I was asking the head of St Agnes's to accept Sarah into his school, Sarah's friends at the School for the Deaf were being taught sign language.

Following this meeting a case conference was held on Sarah's future education. We had asked to be present and our request was refused. We as parents did not qualify for a single vote. We had wanted to give a picture of Sarah's needs as we saw them, and to make a case for her going to St Agnes's school: why it was feasible for her to integrate fully there, and yet not at this stage at her own Junior school.

In time we received a letter to say that a *democratically* agreed decision had been reached. This decision was that Sarah should stay in the Unit until she was eleven when her case would be reviewed again.

It appeared that we as parents held a different view of the needs of our child from that of all the professionals involved. We thought that for a deaf child there may be priorities other than academic ones, *which should for a time take precedence*. The results may not be definable as in reading and writing but they were no less valid. It was precisely *because* Sarah was deaf, that she needed her local school.

The professionals, when it came down to it, knew a lot about Sarah's academic needs but far less about her social and emotional (and her long-term) needs as a deaf child. It was her academic needs they were considering. We were considering Sarah's *whole* needs.

We needed a trial period. We couldn't move without one.

The nightmare was beginning all over again.

* Total Communication is discussed on p. 188.

25. *The wheel goes full circle*

In the school taxi I overheard Sarah and John talking about love and marriage in a way more suited to older children. I heard scuffling and sniggering and though I didn't want to turn round once again, I did.

Anthony was standing with his legs apart making obscene writhing movements. Peter was holding the front of his trousers making equally obscene gestures. On the steamed rear window, obscene pictures had been drawn. Anthony made a two-fingered gesture at the driver behind.

'You rude rude boys,' I said.

The driver must have seen them in his mirror yet he had done nothing to stop them. How long had this sort of thing been going on in the taxi?

When the car stopped the driver said, 'You shouldn't tell them off you know. They don't know any better. Deaf children are different.' Then, when he realized what he had said, he added: 'Except for Sarah of course.'

On arriving home Joanne had an attack of dizziness. Mick had been chasing her upstairs and rolling about with her on the bed when it happened.

We carried her to our room and propped her head high on several pillows. Her face was ashen and her eyes tightly closed. Soon her heart stopped racing and her panic calmed. Mick wiped the perspiration from her forehead with a wet flannel and when Joanne was able to open her eyes a little, I mouthed, 'Joanne, tell me. What is it like?'

'The room is spinning round and round. My head's going round and round.' She whispered from between her teeth as if all movement was unendurable. 'You've got five heads and you're all blurry.'

That night Joanne vomited. She vomited until she was exhausted and then she vomited some more.

Her reeling world continued through the next day and night and, as she couldn't move her head or open her eyes she couldn't read or watch television, and conversation was strictly limited.

At the end of the week Joanne had another, less severe, attack which lasted for two more days.

Everything pointed to Ménière's syndrome, when the fluid in the inner ear becomes distended and affects a person's balance.

'But Joanne never complains,' I said to the specialist. 'As soon as an attack is over she's bright and cheerful again.'

'Yes, but I think children are particularly stoical – I've known huge men collapse like a ton of bricks with it. I'll arrange for Joanne to have some tests.'

These tests cleared Joanne of a brain tumour, the other alternative. Later the worry would have its toll. It appears you can be as strong as it is necessary to be strong but when that need ceases, the strength drains from you leaving only an empty shell. After Joanne's diagnosis I had vowed never to allow myself to feel deeply about anything again. I hadn't been able to escape my grief. It had torn at me from morning till night, when I was making the breakfast, shopping, climbing the stairs. I never wanted to feel as bad as that again.

'Would you mind explaining it to me?' I asked.

'Ménière's has its roots in the inner ear where a fluid called endolymph becomes distended. It can cause damage to the hair cells and this in turn affects the transmission of sound to the nerve of hearing.

'The giddiness is caused by the increase in pressure in the three semi-circular canals which are responsible for balance.'

'Are you saying Joanne's hearing could deteriorate?'

'Damage may occur over a prolonged period to both the hearing and balancing mechanisms.'

'Is there any way we could stop the deterioration from happening?'

'I'll prescribe some medication which has been found to be helpful in reducing the severity of the attacks in some people.'

'But is there a way of avoiding them altogether?'

'You can't protect Joanne from every situation which might trigger an attack. She ought to carry on with the same activities as other children. You could avoid discotheques when she is older though. With the hearing-aid the volume is increased many times over.'

I got up to go. All my fears for Joanne's hearing had been realized.

Once Joanne had an attack during a netball match at school but more often the attacks were triggered by a gradual build-up of tension. Even the most perceptive of teachers couldn't appreciate the variety of pressures Joanne was under, and, as her hearing loss became less and less apparent with her widening experience, it became even harder for them to appreciate it. One teacher said: 'If it wasn't for Joanne's aid we wouldn't think of her as being deaf.'

Then I was grateful for the aid on Joanne's chest. It reminded everyone of her hearing loss and, while I wouldn't want this to mean extra attention necessarily, I did want her deafness to be always considered and that no one be lulled into a false sense of security.

Any situation which involved more than one person speaking made demands upon Joanne. A question behind her: she turns, too late. An answer to the side: she turns again, too late. A voice speaks: Joanne searches the room for the source. Her friend beside her replies: Joanne understands as any child present. The mistake many make is in assuming that, because Joanne hears most things (hears and lipreads), she hears everything. It is not what Joanne hears that counts. It is what she *does not* hear that matters to her.

Without her hearing-aid that would be almost everything. It is certain that had she continued using the one she had first been issued with, she would not be in this school, would have limited language and poor speech, and would not even begin to glimpse the opportunities which now stretch before her without limit.

If all is taken into account – the auditory training unit and the radio-telemetry aid – it is seen that Joanne has received constant amplification of a high quality over a reasonable length of time, and that now we are seeing the results.

The wheel has gone full circle – and yet this is not quite true. Joanne has probably achieved more socially, emotionally, intellectually, and even physically, because she was born a deaf, and not a hearing, child.

'Joanne, are there times when you don't hear the children at school?' I asked.

'Lots of times.'

'What do you do? Do you ask the children what they've said?'

'No, I pretend I've heard. If Zoë is there she always explains.'

We walked on hand in hand. 'Mummy, will I be deaf when I grow up?'

I carried on walking, having left a heart-beat behind. 'Yes you will be deaf when you grow up.'

'Why was I born deaf?'

'You know you have green eyes like me and thick hair like Daddy, well they were passed on to you in your genes. Genes are like messages which tell you are going to be like when you are born. Daddy had a certain gene and I had a certain gene, which together made it likely that our babies would be born with deafness.'

Mick and I had been to see a genetic counsellor who told us we both carried a recessive deafness gene which gave us a one-in-four chance of having a deaf child. When Sarah and Joanne married they would have the same chance as everyone else of having hearing children unless they too married someone with a recessive deafness gene.

'Did you know about it?'

'No, we only found out about it when you were two.'

'Do you want me to be deaf?'

'Did I want you to be deaf you mean. I wanted you just the way you are. I wanted you to be like yourself.'

It was a quiet moment. Joanne was the most extraordinary generous human being. She questioned me gently, stopping when she sensed I might not want to answer, or even it seemed, when it might hurt me too.

'Well Sarah and I could go to Fatima to have our deaffiness cured. Can I have an ice-cream?'

First Year Juniors. Mrs Atkinson

I admit I was apprehensive about having Joanne in my class as I was afraid I might not 'get through' to her and in consequence she would fall behind in her work.

However my fears have proved groundless. Joanne has proved to be highly intelligent and most of the time I am not conscious that she is different from the other children.
Communication.

Apparently no difficulty in communicating with the other children. Appears to understand and be understood. Never seen to be alone at play-times, always included in the group.

Joanne is extremely adept at observation and adapting to what the others are doing when she hasn't heard: in games, outdoor activities and PE for instance.

She concentrates intensely when she isn't hearing and

has a most appealing expression when she is concentrating hard.

On other occasions Joanne daydreams when there is no need for sustained concentration or when the class is working individually. Perhaps this is a kind of relief from the strain of concentration.

Personality.

Joanne is a delightful happy child. She loves to help in class. She is scatter-brained, invariably loses an article of clothing when dressing after PE but very self-reliant in coping with aids.

Apparently no complex about her handicap. One letter she wrote in a class activity began.

'My name is Joanne like you, but I am deaf.'

Work.

Normal development. No evidence at all of handicap.

Works with the top group for everything. If anything a bias towards language work. Joanne is extremely imaginative. She has remarkable comprehension.

Joanne reads with a group of four other girls. They pass the microphone around when reading aloud so that she can follow. She contributes to group work and helps others as much as they help her. No allowances are made for her – the children treat her as any other child, and accept her totally.

Speech.

Tends to be phonetic in pronunciation. For example she sounds 'ed' as 'e-d'.

Music.

Joanne is unable to pitch her voice correctly for singing. However her music teacher was very thrilled to discover that Joanne was able to play the recorder.

26.   *Like bees buzzing*

'Mummy I wan to catch the busder by myself,' Sarah announced.

'You want to catch the bus by yourself do you? I can drop you off in the town and you and Joanne can catch the bus back if you like.'

By midday I had finished my shopping and suggested that Sarah and Joanne buy themselves a cake for tea. At the counter Sarah pointed to a sponge cake and said to the assistant, 'Is it fresh cream?'

I stepped back to see how Sarah would cope if the assistant said 'Pardon'.

'It's fresh cream,' the assistant replied without hesitation.

My satisfaction was complete. Sarah, who for all her life had needed someone, no longer needed me.

Joanne asked for her cake too and afterwards we walked to the bus stop. Sarah was wearing the pink T-shirt we had bought her for her eighth birthday with tiny embroidered flowers around the neckline. Her hair was swept to one side and at the front it was naturally wavy. Her teeth had grown white and straight and with her ready smile were her best feature. She was in fits of giggles because she had stuck a label on Joanne's back with £2.99p written on it.

Joanne was putting on weight, it was her turn to have gaps in her teeth, and her hair was caught back from her face with ribbons. Apart from two tiny marks left by chicken-pox, her complexion was only marred by chocolate around her mouth and a line of ink from Sarah's ballpoint pen. Her face, if not always clean, was sweet and reflected a certain susceptibility.

'Now don't get on the bus unless it's a 264,' I reminded them.

I left them happily clutching their fares and walked to the car but, when I looked towards the bus stop again, there were two buses standing there. I ran as fast as I could and found Sarah on the steps of one of the buses with Joanne frantically tugging at her skirt.

'Please don't get on Sarah,' she was pleading. 'It's the wrong bus. Oh please don't Sarah.'

I held her tight. 'It's all right Jo, it is the right bus. Come on Sarah we're going home in the car.' This independence thing was too nerve-racking for me.

'I'm going on the busder,' Sarah said firmly.

When the bus moved down the High Street I went to the car with Joanne and then drove along a road running parallel to it.

'Can you see the bus Joanne?' I asked, at the point where the High Street ended and the two roads converged.

'No, it's not there.'

I waited for the bus to appear but as the minutes ticked by, I became uneasy. I put my foot on the accelerator and raced along the coast road with visions of Sarah miles from anywhere going through my mind. When we got home I ran into the house to say to Mick breathlessly, 'It's all my fault. I've lost her on the bus.' Then I heard a giggle. I pushed open the lounge door to see Sarah hiding behind the settee. 'Oh Sarah. When did you get home?'

'Aged ago,' she said coolly.

'Ages ago. You beat us then.'

Sarah usually pronounced her 's' sound as 'sh' or 'd' or 't'. Even so the speech therapist still said, 'I've never heard such good speech in a profoundly deaf child.'

I wondered if, by saying Sarah's speech was good, she meant that with an early diagnosis and decent amplification, it could have been even better. Also Sarah would have benefited from having speech therapy almost from the time her deafness was diagnosed because it aimed to help develop language as well as foster good speech patterns.

The audio-physicist at the hospital seemed to think the answer lay in the amplification. 'I don't know whether it was instinct or intuition,' he had said, 'but by providing radio-telemetry aids you did the right thing at the right time.'

It hadn't been instinct or intuition but plain common sense.

'Say Ssss,' I said to Sarah that night as the speech therapist had shown me to do. 'Make it a long, drawn-out sound.'

'Shhh.'

'Put your tongue behind your teeth instead of on the roof of your mouth. Sssss like a snake.' I ran Sarah's finger down the back of a snake I had drawn.

'Ssssshhhh.'

'Once more Sarah.'

Sarah put her tongue behind her teeth. 'Ssss.'

She knew she had done it right immediately, and her face broke into a huge smile.

I collapsed on the bed. 'Sarah you're the cleverest girl in the world. Well done. You did it. Nobody else but you.'

Sarah couldn't stop smiling.

'Right once more. Can you put the "ss" into the word sun?' I wrote it for her.

'Stun.'

'Try breaking it up. "Ss" and "un". Put them together "ssun".

'St . . . un.'

'Let's leave it now. Just do the "ss" once more.'

'Ssss.'

I had many moments of elation with Sarah and yet the feeling was never diminished by this.

I was reading a magazine in the lounge an hour later, and enjoying the peace, when I heard screaming and the sound of running feet. Suddenly the door burst open and Sarah ran into the room white and breathless.

'I heard noised,' she said distractedly. 'I thought it was a burglar but it wasn't.'

I pulled her on to my knee. 'Sarah. What sort of noises?'

'Like bees buzzing and screaming.'

'Have you had them before?'

'Yes lots of times.'

'But why didn't you tell me Sarah?' I asked as a thought occurred to me. 'Did you think it was normal, that everyone heard them?'

'I didn't know it wasn't right.' She shrugged her shoulders.

'How long have you had them?'

''Pose since about four or three.'

'Do you mean since you were a baby?'

She nodded.

'Describe the noises to me.'

'I see dots like bees and big lights with all red round the outside. I can't stand it.'

'When is it worst?'

'At night-time when I've got my hearing-aid off.'

'Would it help it you left your hearing-aid on at bedtime?'

'I'll go straight to sleep then the noises will go away.'

So that was why she had stopped fighting sleep when she was

younger. It was the realization that if she went to sleep the noises went away.

'Is there a noise now?'

Sarah stopped to listen. 'I don't know, I haven't got my hearing-aid on.' Leaning forward she put her ear next to mine. 'Can you hear them?'

I listened to oblige her – and we both burst out laughing.

I realized it was *Tinnitus* – and had always been.

Even from her earliest days she had been jumpy, but not in a nervous way, and unpredictable. One day she had cried with barely a pause for breath. She wanted milk but after taking long sucks, she jumped as if someone was behind her, turned round, gave a cry, began sucking again, whimpering all the time and waving her clenched fists in the air. Then she stopped sucking, twisted her head from side to side, and the whole procedure started again. I could never feed her and put her down. Nothing I did seemed to be right. It was as if she needed something I couldn't provide. The tension in her was unrelenting. It sapped every ounce of my energy. Her screams were chillingly high, determined, never-ending.

Now that I knew it was Tinnitus, I wondered if the droning sound she used to make in her throat had been an attempt to 'mask' the screaming noises in her head. Tinnitus could explain why she used to clench her fists against her head, bang her head against the wall until her forehead was like a band of steel. Why she had fought bed-times and resisted sleep. . . . Could the Tinnitus have been made worse by the emotional disturbance and the emotional disturbance aggravated by the Tinnitus?

Oh Sarah.

27. *The great divide*

'Peak Tarah Bobbins,' a voice on the other end of the telephone said.

'HELLO ANDREA. SARAH'S COMING . . . Mick,' I called. 'Will you tell Sarah to come. Andrea's on the phone.'

Mick told Sarah and she came running into the hall to take the receiver from me.

'Hello Andrea,' she said. 'I'm home. Are you at home? I'm having my tea now. Are you having your tea now? Have you done your homework? I haven't done my homework. See you tomorrow at school. Goodbye for now,' and she calmly replaced the receiver satisfied she had conducted herself well.

As Andrea was also deaf, neither child would have heard what the other one said and, as far as I know, Andrea was still talking long after Sarah had replaced the receiver.

The phone calls were to last about a week and then they stopped altogether. Presumably Sarah and Andrea realized they weren't making much progress. Still they had made their point. They were grown-up now.

When we had first had the telephone installed, Sarah had been puzzled by our one-sided conversations. Then, when she discovered that another person was involved, she wanted to know all about this thing 'conversation' and how it was performed.

She obviously imagined that there was a right way to say something, at a right time, just as once she had decided that people behaved in a certain way, nothing would change her mind. This was why it had been so important that she learn acceptable behaviour before unacceptable behaviour became a permanent fixture in her mind. This inflexibility characterizes much of a deaf child's thinking and serves to make the world seem one large and uncompromising place. Letters to relatives were signed with a formal 'Yours Sincerely Sarah Louise Robinson', which in time had become 'With Love from your darling Sarah Louise

Robinson', to finally, and with much persuasion, 'Love from your darling Sarah'. (She knew 'darling' came into it somewhere.) In much the same way Sarah's first telephone conversation had been conducted something like this: 'Hello Granma are you well? I am well I hope to see you soon I love you goodbye,' and she put down the receiver.

'I wan to be a teacher of the deaf,' Sarah said, not long after her telephone conversation with Andrea ceased.

'But Sarah you can't be a teacher of the deaf,' Joanne replied. 'You won't understand what the children say.'

'Yes I will.'

'Why do you want to be a teacher of the deaf Sarah?' I asked, thinking I've got through to this child at last. She wants to do something for someone else.

'Because', Sarah answered smartly, 'we have a carpet in our classroom and they haven't.'

In bed that night, I thought about what Sarah had said. It had been pure one-upmanship. They might be deaf but *they* had a carpet. The other children might be hearing but *they* hadn't a carpet.

It was also a sign of the great divide.

Sarah, like all other children, had to feel she belonged. The hearing children belonged to their class, and identified with the children in it. Sarah had integrated into the same 'hearing' class since she was six years old, and yet she did not feel she belonged to it. She belonged in the Unit and identified with the children in it. Her expectations were their expectations, their expectations were the expectations of deaf children.

No matter how long Sarah stayed at the Unit she would never identify with the hearing children nor become their friends in the way deaf children had become her friends. Not even if she integrated fully. Sarah would always feel an outsider in the hearing class.

In this way the Unit was a failure.

It was necessary for Sarah to identify with hearing children because one day she was going to live with hearing people. Whatever happened Sarah must not feel like an outsider.

In another way the Unit was a success.

It had prepared Sarah for the transition to a hearing school. We had to help her with that transition. The timing of the move was crucial.

St Agnes's would give Sarah a sense of belonging, not just to the school, the community too. Only when she was fully part of it, would she find her place as a deaf person in it. And I knew it would work simply because everyone, the staff and the children, wanted to make it work.

It was the attitude that counted above everything.

In March, when Sarah was almost nine, she had an occasional day's holiday from her own school and I asked the Headmaster if he would have her at St Agnes's for the day, and he arranged for Sarah to go into Joanne's classroom and to work alongside her.

This was the first opportunity the staff had had of seeing Sarah in a classroom situation although they were aware of her work through her school exercise-books (and the out-of-school activities they involved Sarah in). One of them said afterwards, 'She astounded us. We were so surprised.'

Somehow the knowledge that the staff were more convinced than ever that Sarah would cope, and that this was the time to move her, made our own position worse.

By now I had sought advice from professionals the length and breadth of the country, but renewed efforts at moving Sarah foundered yet again. 'The professionals know what they are doing,' I was told. We had found ourselves in a battle of power which had little to do with what was best for Sarah.

In June Mick and I were invited to a meeting at the Education Offices but I knew before we went it would be abortive. This meeting was followed by another in which we were not present. Then we received a letter.

The Authority felt a move to mainstream education was not appropriate for Sarah and that it was to her advantage to remain in the Unit for the time being. We had however made progress.

> Bearing in mind your very strong conviction that Sarah should move to mainstream as soon as possible as there are other aspects of her development which you feel a placement at St Agnes's would facilitate, I would want to review the situation in good time to consider the possibility of her attending on a trial basis *for the last year*.

In September arrangements were made for Sarah to integrate into the class of one of the most capable teachers in her own school to give her the best chance of coping in a classroom situation.

The following are that teacher's observations:

Games, swimming, library	– No problems.
PE Dancing	– Intelligently watches others where accoustics are poor. Good participation.
Art	– Rarely manages to follow explanation without visual aid. Always given separate attention immediately following lesson talk to class.
Social studies	– Finds distinct problems listening to the radio. Slow worker. Rarely finishes work.
English/Maths	– Methodical worker. Standard just below average in Maths but average in English. Asks when in difficulty but can rarely follow instruction to class. Presentation fair.
Social	– No problems with children who understand the difficulty and do not resent the extra attention given to Sarah nor the slowness of explanation.
Problems	– Cannot understand speech given clearly but at normal speed.* Once 'lost' has not the concentration to maintain interest but patiently awaits individual explanation.

One term later, a term in which Sarah integrated *full-time*, there was an amazing turn of events. The teacher expressed surprise at Sarah's progress in Maths and English; she showed deliberate concentration in following oral instruction; her reading was of a good standard and she tackled words without being familiar with them; she was a methodical worker and worked quietly and neatly, she tackled homework with enthusiasm. . . .

Yet, despite Sarah's most presentable appearance and kind nature, she has not made any strong relationships with any

---

* Deaf children need time to adjust to a new speaker's lip pattern.

children from the class rather maintaining her friendship with another Unit child. Sarah's behaviour is exemplary even in those 'lost' moments.

I feel Sarah could cope with a normal class situation given a sympathetic teacher and a class of children who fully understand her problems – and that she should certainly benefit socially from attending a school within her own home area.

What had happened between the autumn term in which Sarah integrated into her 'hearing' class part-time and the spring term in which she integrated full-time to have wrought such a change?

I think it was altered expectations.

Once Sarah had become her class teacher's full responsibility, and this was the important feature, that she was his responsibility, she rose to meet his expectation of her. She could not have done this herself. He helped her to change her expectations to those of the other children in the class.

In April we received a letter which stated that arrangements were in hand for Sarah to begin a trial placement at St Agnes's school from Monday 27th April.

28.   *A special place*

Sarah's first day at St Agnes's arrived and she woke me with, 'It's time to get up Mum. Did you hear me when I was getting up?'

She was leaning over me smartly dressed in a royal blue sweater and a dress with a tiny check print.

'Oh yes, I heard you.'

She giggled and whispered, 'Did you say "Shut up" to me?'

I smiled. 'Go and put the kettle on, will you. I'll be down in a minute.'

'I'm not getting up yet,' Joanne said when I went into her room to wake her, and she buried her head under the blankets.

Pulling them away from her I said loudly, 'Get up Joanne.' Then repeated 'GET UP' next to her ear.

Downstairs I saw that Sarah had laid the table and was eating breakfast. I poured coffee and called up to Mick, 'Will you tell Joanne to get up?'

Mick went into her room. When she saw him she put her head under the blankets making sure her ears were covered this time. Mick pulled the blankets back. Joanne buried her head in the pillow. 'Joanne. LOOK AT ME.' He stood for a moment then tickled her. She screamed and turned to look at him.

'Okay Dad. I give in. I'll get up I promise. Tell Mum I'm not wearing that scraggy jumper to school and that's definite.'

Sarah looked up from her cereal. 'Hello Dad,' she said, as Mick walked in the room. 'Tell me about the end of the film last night.'

'Well you know that boy was kidnapped,' Mick said, sitting down beside her and knotting his tie. 'He was taken . . .'

Fifteen minutes later, two trips upstairs to call her, Joanne appeared in the kitchen. Her hair was untidy and her shoes undone. I opened her games bag and found a mangled towel and damp swimming costume.

'Mummy can I wear my small hearing-aids to school?'

Both she and Sarah had acquired high-powered ear-level aids

and when Sarah had first put them on, Joanne stepped back to say, 'Sarah they're really lovely.'

'What do you want to wear them to school for Jo?' Mick asked.

'So all the children will 'mire me.'

'I bet they will admire you too,' (and they did) I said. 'Only for today though and then you wear your radio-aid.'

Joanne pushed her mould into her ear grimacing as she did it. 'Aah,' she said, turning it on. 'AAH . . . It's not working.'

I emptied the box of spares on to the table and Joanne changed the battery in her aid.

'Dad. What's a step-dad?'

'A step-dad Sarah is when someone's mother gets married again. The new father is a step-dad. Why? Who? . . .'

'Dad. What's a step-dad?' Joanne interrupted. 'What's a step-dad Dad?' she giggled.

'Joanne I was talking first. Joanne you're a horrible girl.'

Joanne switched her hearing-aid off. 'I can't hear you Sarah.'

'JOANNE YOU'RE A HORRIBLE . . .'

Joanne shut her eyes.

'Quick Sarah,' Mick said. 'The girls are here for you . . .'

On Thursday, three days after she had started at St Agnes's, Sarah went to the youth club with her new-found friends. 'It's much better now because I know everyone,' she said on her return. 'They're all my friends.'

On Friday I watched as she arrived at the school gates oblivious to her two friends shouting, 'Sarah. Sarah,' from behind. They caught up with her breathlessly and tapped her on each shoulder. As she whirled round she smiled, a smile that lit up her whole face, and her friends formed a semi-circle around her and fell into a sideways step to begin an animated conversation.

By the end of the second week Sarah had been to three parties. Children were calling for her after school, she was going to their houses to play, outings were arranged and the telephone rang constantly.

At tea-times now the table buzzed with conversation. Mick and I sat back and let it flow.

'Sarah. What did you think of dinner today? Were you firsts or seconds?'

'Seconds. It was HORRIBLE. The cudard was cold and lumpy. I had to sit next to James. Not James Baxter who live down the road next to Eileen Johnson, the other James.'

'I know Sarah. He's always interfering in our Four Squares.'

But children can be cruel. When the novelty passed would there be a different story? Then there were the hundred and one things which could not be dismissed. The assemblies, the teacher with a beard (this makes lipreading difficult), the radio broadcasts and the language of maths. And what about the teachers themselves? They were trained for hearing children, to equip them educationally, socially and spiritually, for the next stage, and so it went on.

It was what Sarah needed. All that Sarah needed. By now the staff had realized the special place for her was in their school.

Mick and I could not believe the change in Sarah. Not only was she relaxed, confident, and incredibly happy, but her speech was improving too. Instead of an ordinary school providing more pressures, it was infinitely easier for her. No more was she torn between two worlds. It was one world with one set of expectations. No more pressure to be deaf, no more pressures to be hearing. She only had to be herself.

The pressures upon me also eased. Mick had always spent hours telling Sarah and Joanne about the television programmes, talking to them, reading stories, and taking them all over the place, and he did this even more. It was me who took a back seat. 'Now it's you who gets annoyed,' I laughed, and then: 'I must have been hell to live with.'

Mick smiled. 'Hmm, there's been some improvement.'

'Do you think we'll make it?'

'We can have a try.'

In September Sarah went into the top fourth year class, the last one before the children entered the local Comprehensive school. Her teacher was a down-to-earth, capable and experienced lady who asked the children in the class not to repeat the work Sarah should have been paying attention to herself.

The children immediately responded to her request. Little had the teachers thought when they decided to accept Sarah, that the hand they extended would be rewarded in kind. They had looked at the children with new respect and secret pride as boys and girls alike had taken Sarah into their midst. Even Jonathan who was the slowest child in the class had gone out of his way to explain things to Sarah. 'She's really brought him out of himself,' Sarah's teacher was to tell me later.

Deafness needs consideration, generosity, patience and understanding. These caring qualities the children practised each day were such that any parent or school would desire.

No one commented upon her speech but the first time she read aloud in class the children stopped what they were doing and raised their heads to listen. The next time Sarah read, the work continued and no one raised their head.

Meanwhile, Sarah treated the children with the utmost courtesy, waited to be included and tried not to interrupt conversation, and soon the acceptance of her as just another member of the school had already achieved our aim. In time a firm circle of friends were formed and one in particular, Anna. She was Sarah's willing aid, not because Sarah was deaf, but because they were friends. Once, in assembly, Sarah didn't hear the Headmaster say, 'One more verse only,' and carried on singing after the rest of the school had stopped. Seeing Anna bent double with laughter, Sarah nudged her and raised an eyebrow. 'No one's singing,' Anna mouthed, and after looking around her Sarah burst into fits of giggles too.

Anna was more than a friend to Sarah. She and the other children cut deafness down to size. It was of no consequence to them. There was no doubt, though, that for any one child in Sarah's company for any length of time, it was a strain to repeat, to explain, to talk clearly, and yet they never let her down. They included her. Being included is important for any child, especially a deaf child.

At first Anna, intent on making herself understood, pitched her voice to match Sarah's. This died a natural death *as communication daily became more natural in the way of other children.*

Soon Sarah was picking up new vocabulary at an astonishing rate, dropping her 'h's' and 't's' with the best of them.

'Sarah, it's not ma..er, it's ma*tt*er.'

'Yes. Ma..er.'

The days passed.

It seemed Sarah couldn't be better placed or make more progress than she was doing, but was it enough for the Comprehensive School?

The words of the Head of the School for the Deaf once again sprang to mind. 'If she can cope in a Comprehensive, she'll cope with life.'

Because the Comprehensive *was* a fitting for life.

Halfway through the year the Comprehensive became an important topic of conversation amongst the children and Sarah said eagerly, 'Do you know Mum you can choose your dinners and have chips every day. Maggie says that the bully boys ask you if you can see a blue fish down the toilet and if you say "No" they push your head down it. I think it's 'gusting.' She hesitated. 'Will I be going too? Please. Please. I want to go with Anna and all my friends.'

We had never led Sarah to believe she would be going to the Comprehensive but now I took a calculated gamble. I gave Sarah a goal.

'Sarah, it's not up to Dad or me. If you work really hard and concentrate perhaps you could go with Anna. Really it's up to you and no one else.'

Sarah thought about what I had said . . . and within a week we began to see a difference in her work.

Three months later we were able to tell her that in September she would be going to the Comprehensive with her friends.

'It was you who did it though Sarah,' we told her. 'You're the one who made it possible.'

This year then had been vital for Sarah's future education. Because she was happy socially, she was motivated into reaching for a goal no one thought possible she could attain. She pulled herself up in areas of weakness until she was competing on equal terms with her friends – children who had been able to hear all their lives.

The credit must be shared by her class teacher and of course all that had gone before. She had done her best as I knew she would. Whether it was Sarah's personality, or that she represented a challenge, maybe both, but I had no doubts she would respond to her. I had seen it happen so many times before.

Her lack of specialist training had proved to have a positive side in that she was flexible and open to suggestion. She said it brought a freshness to her teaching and kept her on her toes, which meant the other children benefited too. She stopped to think more often and constantly questioned the methods she used. Her only regret, it seemed, was that the school hadn't had Sarah earlier.

St Agnes's had worked out well for Sarah. All that she had needed was for someone to give her a chance.

Sarah and Joanne were fortunate to have been in that kind of atmosphere. The image they carry, and will throughout life, is one of themselves working, competing, playing and cooperating, not as different people, unequal people, or even hearing-impaired people, but as Sarah and Joanne.

One mother told me her daughter had taught her. 'I always shied away from handicap, not because of repugnance, but unfamiliarity, fear and embarrassment. I couldn't adjust my attitudes because I was segregated as a child, and I believe it put a barrier between us. This will never happen to Marie [her daughter] because she has real understanding through contact. *She accepts difference as normal.*'

St Agnes's has future doctors, politicians, health visitors, education advisers, teachers and ordinary people. They, when they wield their power and make their rules, may do so with compassion, knowledge and most of all, understanding. It is in this enlightened atmosphere that I wish Sarah and Joanne to walk.

On the last day of term the parents were invited to an assembly in the school hall. Sun poured through the windows as the children filed into the hall and class after class joined in the singing until the room was filled with the sound of children's voices.

I looked at Sarah and Joanne standing in their lines, and contentment flowed through me. For the first time since Sarah's diagnosis, I felt at peace. Here Sarah and Joanne had been given the freedom to grow. They had found their place.

They belonged.

Sarah's class teacher

When Sarah first came into my class it must have been as traumatic for her to accept a new teacher as it was for me to accept a handicapped child for the first time.

My main worry was that my inexperience in dealing with a child who had impaired hearing would prevent me from doing justice to Sarah, and that in my care she would not reach her potential. As it was hoped Sarah would go on to the Comprehensive School this would be a crucial year for her. Thus it was with some trepidation that our first term started.

My first thoughts were to treat her as a special case but, on reflection, I decided this would impede her integration – the very reason she had come to a normal classroom teaching situation. So, hard though it may be, I decided to make minimum concession to her disability.

Academically she was behind in Maths, much of the language being unfamiliar to her, but she worked hard (not always willingly), learned her tables, and made excellent progress. Her reading was good, as was her comprehension, and although we discovered words she did not understand,

words long familiar to other children, there were no problems
we couldn't overcome. The backing service I received from
the peripatetic teacher of the deaf (half an hour a week) was
invaluable as she went through work with Sarah before we did
it so she was familiar with the basic idea we were discuss-
ing. Also if anything needed reinforcing she helped with
this.

In oral work Sarah was not in the least inhibited, and the
rest of the class had no difficulty understanding and, indeed,
accepting her. She participated in all school activities, games
being one of her favourite lessons.

The fact that Sarah was such an excellent lipreader certainly facilitated communication, and I soon got used to repeating
answers the children behind her gave. The microphone became a thing of habit too and the Headmaster wore it during
assemblies so Sarah could take an active part.

By the end of the year I had every hope Sarah would hold
her own in the Comprehensive School.

I enjoyed teaching her and got great satisfaction when her
face and eyes lit up with understanding as yet one more
problem was solved, and great misgiving when I had to mete
out criticism of work badly done and watch her eyes fill with
tears perhaps.

I feel she is a fully integrated member of the class, ready to
face the difficulties of life at secondary level, but I feel this was
due, in the main, to the excellent caring instruction she
received in the previous years, and above all to her own
courageous temperament.

She is a happy child, full of fun, confident in her relationships with others. She is not particularly hard-working unless
often cajoled and encouraged, a good runner, a competent
netball player, and an intrepid goalkeeper at hockey.

This was a unique situation involving a group of children
and a body of staff who showed Sarah every sympathy and
understanding, but had this not been so the outcome might
have been different.

In September Sarah started at the Comprehensive School surrounded by her friends from St Agnes's. Sitting beside her in class
was a child who had been born at the same time as she was in the
same Nursing Home. Sarah and Pauline's son, Christopher, had
indeed trodden different paths, Sarah through another world, but

this day in September those paths were joined and together they looked to the future.

The following September Joanne started at the Comprehensive School too: two children with their heads held high.

Epilogue

I have tried to catalogue in this book those factors which are necessary if a child is to become socially, emotionally, and intellectually adjusted, first as an individual and then as a fully integrated person in society. In the process of collating this information I became aware that many of the services which exist to aid and support our children can actually work *against* their development. This led to my writing articles, giving talks, and recording interviews with radio and television. I began to campaign for the early diagnosis of hearing loss and this was raised in Parliament with a view to mandatory testing of babies and the keeping of nationwide records. I followed this by producing a leaflet and poster which have been distributed nationally. It was inevitable that certain opinions have formed in my mind and these have been reinforced by my research and corroborated by evidence culled from letters I received from parents and professionals. I would now like to comment upon these.

The scandal of late diagnosis

Throughout the world many thousands of babies are born every day who will be isolated from sound, and therefore language, for two, three, four or more years, before they receive a diagnosis of their deafness and treatment begins.

Severely deaf children are a small minority of the population (1 in a 1,000 births) compared with markedly more widespread children with partial loss of hearing and children who will suffer minor impairments of hearing in the early stages of life, the effects of which may not become apparent for some time. This last group concerns *all* parents because of the disturbingly high likelihood of their children suffering some form of hearing impairment caused by common ailments.*

* See page 181/182.

Causes of deafness

First type of hearing loss

If sound is halted before it reaches the inner ear it is called a CONDUCTIVE loss and is treated medically. This sort of problem most usually occurs after birth.

Some causes are:

- infections of the tonsils and adenoids
- acute ear infections
- certain common viruses such as measles, influenza, glandular fever
- wax

The most frequent cause of hearing impairment is due to a build-up of fluid in the middle ear (arising from certain of the above conditions) which restricts the movement of the ossicles (three linked bones in the middle-ear) and therefore the passage of sound. If not treated, this can lead to a thickening of the fluid and possible permanent deafness. This is known as SECRETORY OTITIS MEDIA or GLUE EAR.

As the incidence of fluid is high in the early years, a child may not hear, to a greater or lesser extent, in periods crucial to the development of speech and language. This is likely to have far-reaching consequences for linguistic development and school progress.

Once fluid is detected (and the surest way for this to happen is to give routine 'Impedence Audiometry' – a method of discovering fluid – to all pre-school children at the same time as the more usual screening tests and developmental checks), then a child may be kept under observation, receive medical treatment or be referred to the peripatetic service for support and aids for when hearing is particularly depressed.

Second type of hearing loss

If sound reaches the inner ear but, due to a disorder of the Cochlea (or nerve of hearing), does not reach the brain, the hearing loss is SENSORI-NEURAL. The result is always permanent and serious.

Some causes are:

- contact with German measles (rubella) during pregnancy. Rubella virus is the cause of other handicaps beside deafness such as blindness, heart disease and mental deficiency, *all of which are entirely preventable*. Protection against rubella can be given by inoculation.
- difficult birth or shortage of oxygen at birth
- mumps, meningitis
- threatened abortion (threatened miscarriage)
- severe jaundice at birth
- rhesus incompatibility (a disorder of the blood)
- inherited deafness (occurring in families) also includes RECESSIVE DEAFNESS. The deafness gene or trait is passed on by the parents. A high proportion of congenitally deaf children are thought to have recessive deafness. No family history will be present.

The importance of early diagnosis

In the first years of a child's life billions of nerve cells are developing branch-like connections between the different areas of the brain.

All children are born with the potential for language but it seems likely that its development depends upon the density of those branches which connect the areas of the brain concerned – and it seems likely this only occurs with the *experience* of language.

This could explain why it was a monumental task to reverse the effects of deafness in Sarah in order to make her become a child who was responsive to sound and language, and why I felt we reached her only in the nick of time, *before it was too late*.

What can be done?

1. A full-scale propaganda campaign is needed, starting with teenage children in all schools, educating them to the importance of hearing in the development of language and the need for early detection of hearing loss. This campaign should be extended through the media, the distribution of relevant literature, and to ante-natal classes and baby clinics. Parents should be helped to recognize that:

- hearing impairment is possible in their child
- it can be difficult to detect
- deaf and hearing-impaired babies will look 'normal'.
- there are degrees of deafness: a baby may hear sound yet still be hearing-impaired
- a baby could appear to turn to sound but may be responding to some other stimulation such as vibration
- they can request further screening tests if they are worried.

Parents should attend all screening tests for hearing *and* all developmental checks (retarded language development may indicate a possible hearing loss). Deafness can arise any time *before* or *after* these tests so parents should be alert to signs which may indicate a problem.

2. Doctors should listen to parents and not dismiss them as being over-anxious. If parents suspect hearing loss they are usually correct. Training in audiology should be a basic requirement for all doctors: 'I saw four doctors in our practice about John's hearing and they told me I was worrying too much as he was my first baby. I kept thinking the doctors had to be right and John was stubborn.' (Mother of a severely deaf boy)

3. The health visitor's role is vital in the detection of hearing loss. She has the knowledge of the developmental stages of a child and, together with a parents' observations, progress can be monitored through regular home visits.

There may be, considering the difficulties inherent in the identification of hearing loss and the numbers of children involved, reason to have specialism in health visiting: 'My son passed five hearing tests. Some of them my husband and I had demanded since he was ten months old. We were told we were just neurotic. Eventually at twenty-seven months an audiologist pronounced him deaf. Because of the late diagnosis he said our son was unlikely to talk normally.' (Mother). 'Hearing tested. NORMAL.' (Extract from Sarah's medical records at eight months of age).

4. The Government should formulate a national policy, recognized in law, which would give a standardized approach to the screening of hearing for children.

There should be routine screening for hearing *before*, and certainly at, the age of nine months, at about eighteen months, and three years, by trained health visitors. (This infers an agreed policy regarding the training of health visitors and the performance of screening tests.) Consideration should be given to the inclusion of Impedance Audiometry and electronic screening methods in the tests.

Records of screening should be available at a national level with the results monitored and published annually to show the percentage of children tested, referred for diagnostic assessment, and shown to have a hearing loss needing medical and/or educational treatment.

6. There is no national pattern of referral for audiological investigation and waiting lists are often lengthy: 'Urgent matter for Sarah to be referred. Mother thinks she is able to hear after antibiotics. Long history of tonsillitis. She did not hear the tuning-fork by air conduction but did by bone. No speech at all. Answers to signs.' (This was one of several letters sent by the clinic doctor in an attempt to get Sarah examined at an Audiology Clinic).

Long waiting lists for children with Glue Ear bring with them the risk of permanent deafness.

Standardized procedures for referral, or open referral, and the recognition of the need for early diagnosis should contribute to the welfare of deaf and hearing-impaired children.

Hearing-aid provision

Hearing-aids are available to children on the National Health Service and a wide range of government and commercial aids can be prescribed. Regardless of this the provision of aids can sometimes be an indiscriminate affair and this places parents in the unenviable position of not being able to tell with any certainty whether their child's hearing-aid is the most suitable for his type of loss.

Today there are few children with hearing loss who could not benefit in some way from a hearing-aid, and yet many discard them. This may happen if:

- the aid they possess is incorrect or inadequate for their hearing loss; the ear mould does not fit correctly; the aid has not been adjusted to suit their individual needs.
- they were not helped to make full use of their residual

hearing at a time when it would have been most impressionable to auditory stimulation.

In conclusion

Only adequately trained specialists should be involved in the prescribing and fitting of hearing-aids. (This would require the setting-up of special training courses.) Parents should request an 'aided' audiogram and 'aided' speech tests (plus copies of all hearing tests). This means that a child will be tested when wearing his hearing-aid to show the amount of actual help he receives from it. It is more important to know what a child *can* hear with an aid, than to know what he *can't* hear without one.

Ideally a child's response to sound should be assessed for different hearing-aids. When this was done for Sarah and Joanne the results were telling:

Sarah:
- without an aid (at the ear): no discrimination of speech at 115 decibels
- with National Health aids: no discrimination of speech
- with radio-telemetry aids: discrimination at *60–65* decibels

Joanne:
- without an aid (at the ear): discrimination at 90–95 decibels in the right ear and 100–105 decibels in the left ear
- with National Health aids: discrimination at 70 decibels
- with radio-telemetry aid: discrimination at *55–60* decibels

Parents should find out how their child's hearing-aid works, how to check that it is in working order, how to change leads and batteries and make simple repairs.

Parents should learn to ask professionals for information (write the questions down beforehand) and professionals to give that information in such a way that a parent will understand.

All parents should be issued with adequate numbers of spare batteries and leads for both Government and commercial aids.

When hearing-aids need repairing a similar type should be issued temporarily in its place.

If necessary parents should request help with the cost of transport to hospitals and clinics for appointments.

If parents are unhappy about National Health provision or have cause for complaint they can:

- ask for an appointment to see the specialist directly concerned
- contact the specialist in Community Medicine (child health) or the Consumer Health Council who exist to represent consumer interests
- contact their local Deaf Children's Society, the National Deaf Children's Society, or other child welfare groups

Parents should know what it is they want from professionals and ask for it. Often clinicians are unaware of the causes of concern to parents. It is up to us to make them aware.*

Radio-telemetry aids

These have the potential to be one of the directing influences upon the course of deaf children's lives. When children are given access to them in the early years their value is beyond compare.

Some of the benefits over and above that of an ordinary hearing-aid and auditory training unit are:

- they allow parents *immediate* contact with their child
- they allow greater opportunity for auditory stimulation and language stimulation
- they allow a child to receive good quality sound reproduction across a wide range of frequencies at a correct level of amplification
- they allow for the freedom of natural language growth. (They are less restrictive than an auditory training unit)
- they allow a young child to hear and become accustomed to a consistent pattern of sound which is continued in schools where radio-telemetry aids are provided

Some of the benefits to Sarah and Joanne were:

- an improvement in their responses to sound and in the quality of their speech.

* With acknowledgement to the National Deaf Children's Society for their booklet, *Deaf children and their hearing-aids*.

- in allowing them access to mainstream education. (Not that mainstream education is a measure of success. It all depends on a child's specific needs [and education facilities available] at any given time. A special school or unit is infinitely preferable to placement in mainstream education if it invites failure for whatever reason e.g. inadequate backing or insufficient equipment). In Sarah and Joanne's cases the saving on special education facilities was many thousands of pounds
- in allowing their teachers direct contact with them in the classroom

While radio-telemetry aids remain the best source of amplification for most (but not all) deaf children, there are drawbacks.

- the cost is prohibitive for many parents. One man sold his house to raise funds to buy his child such an aid
- repairs take time and are expensive

Education Authorities provide this type of hearing system in many schools and units but it is still not generally recognized that the child most likely to receive maximum benefit from it has yet to begin school. Occasionally forward-thinking health authorities provide these aids for pre-school children on the National Health Service but these are rare. Others are being provided by charities such as the National Deaf Children's Society and organizations like the Round Table.

The 1981 Education Act requires health and education authorities to cooperate closely over the assessment of children with special needs, and to make provision for those children who require special equipment to meet those needs.

This *should* include the provision of radio-telemetry aids wherever this is practically possible, and the Department of Health and Social Security are aware of this.

Ear moulds

The situation regarding the production of ear moulds for children is as grave now as it ever was. I cannot think of another cause of so much frustration and this is echoed by parents every day: 'We have tried to get decent-fitting ear moulds through the National Health

Service ever since our daughter's deafness was diagnosed, and we have dozens of ear moulds in the drawer to prove it.' (Mother)

A close-fitting ear mould is the *first* consideration for a deaf child. It is possible to obtain them for young children but it is a task requiring patience and skill.

Health Authorities should provide facilities where suitably trained staff are available to use nationally recommended materials and methods in the making of ear moulds.

Parents should *persist* in trying to obtain adequate ear moulds until they are satisfied that the ones they receive allow the recommended amplification to be used on their child's hearing-aid. Speed is of utmost importance with young children whose ears are growing, therefore needing a succession of ear moulds.

Total Communication

Approximately 95 per cent of parents of deaf children are themselves hearing people and yet, within a few days of finding out their child is deaf, they may be faced with learning a new language: sign language. In England the Oral method of communication has reigned supreme in the education of deaf children. In recent years this supremacy has been challenged.

By its very existence Total Communication suggests that Oralism does not, indeed cannot, meet the needs of all deaf children and this accounts for their low level of academic achievement. Total Communication purports to raise these standards and on the face of it such a philosophy does have a good chance of doing this because, through sign language, communication is made easy. Ease of communication is crucial to any child's success.

Some Total Communicationalists believe that over a certain level of hearing loss, 85 decibels, children do not benefit to any significant extent from their hearing and that lipreading is an inadequate means of gaining information, as only a certain percentage of words are distinguishable on the lips. If this is true, the *primary* way of gaining information in a Total Communication environment for these children must be through sign language.

Under an Oralist system there are children who have not prospered, but what proportion of these have had a late diagnosis, little or no pre-school help, inadequate hearing-aids, ill-fitting ear moulds, wrong school placements or poor teaching? Or no additional support such as Cued Speech (the 'cueing' of certain sounds by hand signals)? Have these things proved too great a barrier for children to develop in the way they may have done had their paths not been littered with just too many obstacles to overcome? If this is the case the principle of Oralism may not be at fault but rather the carrying out of that principle.

There are undoubtedly children who need sign language, but how are they to be identified? When they have failed to become oral, or from the time their deafness is diagnosed?

Total Communicationalists aim to reach all educationally severely and profoundly deaf children from the earliest opportunity (and may encompass children with partial hearing losses too).

This places parents in the unenviable position of having to decide which is the best way of communicating with their six-month-old baby or two-year-old child, and having the tenacity to follow that decision through, even when it may go against current practice in their particular area. This applies to both philosophies.

But perhaps parents can turn this to their advantage by taking from the different philosophies what *they* want for *their child* at any given time. It may be that they use Total Communication until their child has a basic language. (The philosophy of TC being that sign language is used in a purely supportive role, i.e., to promote oral language skills).* Or they can use Total Communication all the time. Or they may decide to concentrate their efforts on purely Oral methods. They may decide to use Cued Speech to support the Oral method, or, later on, finger-spelling. Whatever decision they come to, and it may be different decisions at different times, it may not be the method used once their child reaches school. This could lead to incompatibility between school and home.

What parents will have to consider, or monitor, with Total Communication is how much their child grows to *depend* on the signing side of the communication.

To digress a moment. When Sarah and Joanne were first diagnosed as deaf, they were given hearing-aids for their right ears only and they learned to *depend* upon those ears to hear. Later, when hearing-aids were provided for their left ears and stimulation given, it was found to be too late. Their left ears were virtually

---

* Certainly I would have used sign language with Sarah in the early stages as a means of clarifying the spoken word, and then gradually dropped it as the need for it lessened. (In much the same way as mothers of hearing children drop natural gesture). I would also have expended more energy developing Sarah's listening skills.

non-functional despite their being *very little* difference in the actual hearing loss between their right and left ears.

What should be considered with Total Communication then, is whether the primary means of gaining information (sign language) will *decrease* a child's dependency upon hearing and lipreading and, instead, become the natural means of acquiring information, or will actually *aid* this process.

But whatever parents *choose* in the way of communication with their child, his progress will ultimately depend upon their belief in him being able to achieve (whatever the method or methods used) and the amount of effort they then give to it. It is about belief – and of course many other things as well. And if we do not have the belief, and if the National Health Service, the Education Service and the Social Services are unwilling to provide those ingredients which are fundamental to the success of a deaf child, then we will have children leaving school with limited comprehension skills, unintelligible speech, and illiterate, to be thrust into a world of hearing people as a permanent reminder of our abysmal failure, as has happened in the past and – dare I say it – still happens now.

Useful addresses

THE NATIONAL DEAF CHILDREN'S SOCIETY

45 Hereford Road
London W2 5AH

THE ROYAL NATIONAL INSTITUTE FOR THE DEAF

105 Gower Street
London WC1E 6AH

THE BRITISH DEAF ASSOCIATION

38 Victoria Place
Carlisle CA1 1EX

THE BRITISH ASSOCIATION OF THE HARD OF HEARING

7–11 Armstrong Road
Acton
London W3 7JL

THE BREAKTHROUGH TRUST

Charles Gillett Centre
Selly Oak Colleges
Birmingham B29 6LE